Friends of the
Houston Public Library

Walter Dean Myers

WHO WROTE THAT?

LOUISA MAY ALCOTT	PAT MORA	E.B. WHITE
JANE AUSTEN	WALTER DEAN MYERS	LAURA INGALLS WILDER
AVI	SCOTT O'DELL	
JUDY BLUME	BARBARA PARK	LAURENCE YEP
BETSY BYARS	GARY PAULSEN	JANE YOLEN
MEG CABOT	TAMORA PIERCE	
BEVERLY CLEARY	EDGAR ALLAN POE	
ROBERT CORMIER	BEATRIX POTTER	
BRUCE COVILLE	PHILIP PULLMAN	
ROALD DAHL	MYTHMAKER: THE STORY OF J.K. ROWLING	
CHARLES DICKENS		
THEODOR GEISEL		
WILL HOBBS	MAURICE SENDAK	
ANTHONY HOROWITZ	SHEL SILVERSTEIN	
GAIL CARSON LEVINE	GARY SOTO	
C.S. LEWIS	R.L. STINE	
ANN M. MARTIN	EDWARD L. STRATEMEYER	
L.M. MONTGOMERY		

Walter Dean Myers

Amy Sickels

**Foreword by
Kyle Zimmer**

An imprint of Infobase Publishing

Walter Dean Myers

Copyright © 2008 by Infobase Publishing

All rights reserved. No part of this book may be reproduced or utilized in any form or by any means, electronic or mechanical, including photocopying, recording, or by any information storage or retrieval systems, without permission in writing from the publisher. For information contact:

Chelsea House
An imprint of Infobase Publishing
132 West 31st Street
New York NY 10001

Library of Congress Cataloging-in-Publication Data
Sickels, Amy.
  Walter Dean Myers / Amy Sickels.
    p. cm. — (Who wrote that?)
  Includes bibliographical references and index.
  ISBN 978-0-7910-9524-9 (hardcover : acid-free paper) 1. Myers, Walter Dean, 1937—Juvenile literature. 2. Authors, American—20th century—Biography—Juvenile literature. 3. African American authors—Biography—Juvenile literature. 4. Young adult literature—Authorship—Juvenile literature. I. Title. II. Series.
  PS3563.Y48Z85 2008
  813'.54—dc22
  [B]   2007045507

Chelsea House books are available at special discounts when purchased in bulk quantities for business, associations, institutions, or sales promotions. Please call our Special Sales Department in New York at (212) 967-8800 or (800) 322-8755.

You can find Chelsea House on the World Wide Web at http://www.chelseahouse.com

Text design by Keith Trego and Erika K. Arroyo
Composition by EJB Publishing Services
Cover design by Keith Trego and Jooyoung An
Cover printed by Yurchak Printing, Landisville, Pa.
Book printed and bound by Yurchak Printing, Landisville, Pa.

Printed in the United States of America

This book is printed on acid-free paper.

All links and Web addresses were checked and verified to be correct at the time of publication. Because of the dynamic nature of the Web, some addresses and links may have changed since publication and may no longer be valid.

Table of Contents

FOREWORD BY
KYLE ZIMMER
PRESIDENT, FIRST BOOK 6

1 FILLING THE VOID 11

2 TROUBLE WITH WORDS 19

3 DROPPING OUT 35

4 A CHILDREN'S STORY 47

5 FULL-TIME WRITER 57

6 ENDLESS IDEAS 65

7 TEENS IN HARLEM 75

8 CRITICAL ACCLAIM 85

9 DISCIPLINE, DEDICATION, AND FUN 93

CHRONOLOGY 103
NOTES 105
WORKS BY WALTER DEAN MYERS 108
POPULAR BOOKS 110
POPULAR CHARACTERS 113
MAJOR AWARDS 116
BIBLIOGRAPHY 119
FURTHER READING 121
INDEX 123

FOREWORD BY
KYLE ZIMMER
PRESIDENT, FIRST BOOK

HUMANITY IS POWERED by stories. From our earliest days as thinking beings, we employed every available tool to tell each other stories. We danced, drew pictures on the walls of our caves, spoke, and sang. All of this extraordinary effort was designed to entertain, recount the news of the day, explain natural occurrences—and then gradually to build religious and cultural traditions and establish the common bonds and continuity that eventually formed civilizations. Stories are the most powerful force in the universe; they are the primary element that has distinguished our evolutionary path.

Our love of the story has not diminished with time. Enormous segments of societies are devoted to the art of storytelling. Book sales in the United States alone topped $24 billion in 2006; movie studios spend fortunes to create and promote stories; and the news industry is more pervasive in its presence than ever before.

There is no mystery to our fascination. Great stories are magic. They can introduce us to new cultures or remind us of the nobility and failures of our own; inspire us to greatness or scare us to death; but above all, stories provide human insight on a level that is unavailable through any other source. In fact, stories connect each of us to the rest of humanity not just in our own time, but also throughout history.

FOREWORD

This special magic of books is the greatest treasure that we can hand down from generation to generation. In fact, that spark in a child that comes from books became the motivation for the creation of my organization, First Book, a national literacy program with a simple mission: to provide new books to the most disadvantaged children. First Book has been at work in hundreds of communities for over a decade. Every year, children in need receive millions of books through our organization, and millions more are provided through dedicated literacy institutions across the United States and around the world. In addition, groups of people dedicate themselves tirelessly to working with children to share reading and stories in every imaginable setting from schools to the streets. Of course, this Herculean effort serves many important goals. Literacy translates to productivity and employability in life and many other valid and even essential elements. But at the heart of this movement are people who love stories, love to read, and want desperately to ensure that no one misses the wonderful possibilities that reading provides.

When thinking about the importance of books, there is an overwhelming urge to cite the literary devotion of great minds. Some have written of the magnitude of the importance of literature. Amy Lowell, an American poet, captured the concept when she said, "Books are more than books. They are the life, the very heart and core of ages past, the reason why men lived and worked and died, the essence and quintessence of their lives." Others have spoken of their personal obsession with books, as in Thomas Jefferson's simple statement: "I live for books." But more compelling, perhaps, is the almost instinctive excitement in children for books and stories.

Throughout my years at First Book, I have heard truly extraordinary stories about the power of books in the lives of children. In one case, a homeless child, who had been bounced from one location to another, later resurfaced—and the only possession that he had fought to keep was the book he was given as part of a First Book distribution months earlier. More recently, I met a child who, upon receiving the book he wanted, flashed a big smile and said, "This is my big chance!" These snapshots reveal the true power of books and stories to give hope and change lives.

As these children grow up and continue to develop their love of reading, they will owe a profound debt to those volunteers who reached out to them—a debt that they may repay by reaching out to spark the next generation of readers. But there is a greater debt owed by all of us—a debt to the storytellers, the authors, who have bound us together, inspired our leaders, fueled our civilizations, and helped us put our children to sleep with their heads full of images and ideas.

WHO WROTE THAT? is a series of books dedicated to introducing us to a few of these incredible individuals. While we have almost always honored stories, we have not uniformly honored storytellers. In fact, some of the most important authors have toiled in complete obscurity throughout their lives or have been openly persecuted for the uncomfortable truths that they have laid before us. When confronted with the magnitude of their written work, we can forget that writers are people. They struggle through the same daily indignities and dental appointments, and they experience the intense joy and bottomless despair that

FOREWORD

many of us do. Yet, somehow they rise above it all to weave a powerful thread that connects us all. It is a rare honor to have the opportunity that these books provide to share the lives of these extraordinary people. Enjoy.

Walter Dean Myers is the acclaimed author of over 80 books, including Fallen Angels, The Glory Field, *and* Monster.

1

Filling the Void

IN 1968, WALTER Dean Myers heard about a children's book contest for African-American writers. Before this, he had never thought about writing a children's book, even though he loved to write. Myers had been writing poems and short stories since he was a child. Now he was a father of two and was working a full-time job at the U.S. Post Office to support his family. At night, his only free time, he wrote articles and short stories for adults. He thought hard about whether he could write a children's story for the contest and decided to give it a shot.

For his submission, Myers wrote a story called *Where Does the Day Go?* about an African-American father who takes his son and a few neighborhood kids on a walk to the park. Each child wonders where the sun goes at the end of the day. The children give their explanations, and at the end of the story, the father tells them what actually happens when the sun sets. Myers was thrilled when he found out that he won first place. The story was published as a book by *Parents' Magazine* and became a hit among children, parents, and librarians.

Myers enjoyed writing the story and thought he would write more for children. He had no idea that it was the start of productive writing career. He did not know that one day he would become one of the country's most respected writers for children and young adults.

Since the publication of *Where Does the Day Go?* Myers has published more than 80 books for children and young adults and has received many prestigious awards for his work. He is a five-time winner of the Coretta Scott King Award for African-American writers and has been chosen for the Newbery Honor Book Award twice.

Nobody from Myers's childhood, including Myers himself, could have predicted this kind of success. Though he loved to read and write as a child, actually making a living as a writer seemed like a fantasy, an unattainable dream.

Myers grew up in Harlem during World War II. His loving foster parents struggled financially to provide a stable home for Walter. He loved his family and his neighborhood. School, however, was not easy. Walter found it difficult to concentrate in class, and he also struggled with a speech problem. Teachers and other kids had trouble understanding him. He turned to books for escape. Reading took him to other places and showed him other worlds. It seemed natural that he would also turn to writing. Writing gave him license to explore his imagination. He spent much of his time with his nose in a book or with a pencil in his hand.

Despite this early interest in writing, Walter never thought that one day he would write for a living. He may have sometimes imagined this, but he did not know how he could make this dream a reality. In his life, there were no role models, no examples of how to become a writer. Most of the authors Walter read were dead white men, and the few living authors that he read were also white. He did not read many books by African-American writers or stories about African-American children. He never saw himself or his community portrayed in the books that he read.

Myers did not go to college after high school. In fact, he did not even finish high school. He joined the army. After he was discharged, he worked at many different jobs, in various places, including factories and the post office. He wrote whenever he could find the time.

After *Where Does the Day Go?* Myers published two more picture books. Six years later, he wrote his first novel for young adults. It was called *Fast Sam, Cool Clyde, and Stuff.* Writing this novel was a major turning point in his life. He realized that he had found his calling.

For this book, Myers turned to his personal memories of growing up in Harlem and transformed them into fiction. Some of his own experiences from childhood influenced the story line, and his son inspired the character of Stuff. Set in Harlem on 116th Street, the novel follows 12-year-old Francis, called Stuff, and two older boys, athletic Sam and thoughtful Clyde. The boys, along

WALTER DEAN MYERS

Printz Award—winning Author of MONSTER

WALTER DEAN MYERS

SHOOTER

Myers's popular and critically acclaimed novel Shooter is about young people, violence, and guns. Myers was inspired to write the book after the tragedy at Columbine High School.

FILLING THE VOID

with 14-year-old Gloria, form a group called the Good People. As the young teens face difficult problems—family breakups, drugs, poverty—they turn to each other for support and protection. There are many humorous and lighthearted scenes in the book, but Myers also depicts many harsh realities to which a kid living in Harlem might be able to relate. For example, racism is evident when the cops mistakenly accuse the boys of crime, assuming they are guilty because of the color of their skin.

Did you know...

Actor and director Debbi Allen asked Myers to write a children's book based on the incident of *La Amistad*. In 1839, 53 Africans who had been captured to be sold into slavery mutinied on board the ship *La Amistad*. They were successful and later the U.S. Supreme Court declared the revolt legitimate. The Africans were returned to Freetown, a settlement for freed slaves in Sierra Leone. Debbi Allen was captivated by the story of the revolt, and she vowed to bring the tale to the big screen. The movie *Amistad* (1997), produced by Allen and directed by Steven Spielberg, stars many famous actors, including Morgan Freeman. For the book, *Amistad: A Long Road to Freedom*, Myers gives a dramatic, factual account of the story, including maps, schedules, a time line, and photographs.

Myers, today a father of three and a grandfather, lives in Jersey City, New Jersey, with his wife, Connie. He travels around the world to research his books, but he also finds inspiration in old photographs, letters, family stories, and historical events. Harlem again and again provides Myers with source material because he is able to draw on his own experiences and observations there.

Myers is a prolific writer. He has published biographies, fairy tales, ghost stories, history books, picture books, and adventure stories, but he is best known for his realistic novels that explore the lives of African-American teenagers living in Harlem. "No one has given his readers more truth in his portrayal of young blacks struggling with tough life choices and conflicting values," writes editor Tom Reynolds.[1] Myers does not shy away from writing about the challenging realities that face today's urban youth, as his characters struggle to survive drug-riddled streets, racist police, and violent gangs.

Myers feels that it is important for African-American youth to see reflections of themselves and their communities in books. He realized early on in his career that he wanted to provide young people with the kind of books that he never encountered when he was a kid—realistic, truthful books about African-American experiences. He has challenged publishers to put out more African-American literature and also encouraged libraries and parents to support these books. Though many more African-American authors are published today than when Myers was growing up, there continues to be an absence of the black experience in contemporary young adult literature. Myers has done his best to change this.

FILLING THE VOID

Through his persistence, dedication, and love for writing, Myers has become one of today's most popular and critically acclaimed writers for young adults. With his vivid, character-driven novels, Myers reaches a large audience of diverse readers, including isolated teens, and helps to bridge the gaps between the races.

Walter Dean Myers grew up in Harlem in the 1940s, under the care of his foster parents, Florence Brown Dean and Herbert Dean. The photograph above was taken in the 1960s on a typical street in Harlem.

2

Trouble With Words

WALTER DEAN MYERS moved to Harlem, where many of his stories and books take place, when he was three years old. For the first three years of his life, he lived in the industrial town of Martinsburg, West Virginia. Martinsburg is located in the eastern panhandle of the state, near Harper's Ferry, the site of the John Brown raid of 1859. John Brown was an abolitionist, meaning that he opposed slavery. He and about 20 followers decided to raid the federal arsenal (store of weapons) at Harper's Ferry in order to arm the slaves and lead an uprising. They were captured in the process, and Brown was put on trial for treason. Some of Myers's ancestors lived at Harper's Ferry, and according to family legend, his great-great-great uncle, a slave, saw John Brown on his way to trial.

Walter was born many years later to George Ambrose Myers and Mary Dolly Green Myers on August 12, 1937. Walter had five older siblings: Geraldine, Ethel, Viola, Gertrude, and George. The Myers family lived in a small, crowded house, and the parents struggled to make ends meet and to feed their children. When Walter turned three, his mother died while giving birth to his sister, Imogene. Walter was suddenly left with only one parent.

This was during the Great Depression, a major economic recession that spanned the years from 1929 to 1941. The Great Depression is usually thought of as beginning on Black Tuesday, October 29, 1929, when the stock market crashed. The crash led to massive bank failures and high unemployment around the country. Work was difficult to come by, especially for African Americans. Racism was everywhere; when jobs occasionally became available, they were usually given to white men. At this time, West Virginia was segregated, and African-American employees were the first to be laid off. African Americans not only struggled through the Depression but also bore the heavy weight of racial discrimination in the workforce and society.

Walter's father suddenly found himself responsible for raising six children and the new baby on his own. Friends and family helped out when they could, bringing over food and watching the youngest children. Their support was not enough. George Myers did not know how he would earn a living and care for his large family without help.

George Myers spoke with his first wife, Florence Brown Dean, the mother of Walter's half sisters, Geraldine and

TROUBLE WITH WORDS

Viola. After the divorce, Dean had remarried and moved to New York. Dean was the daughter of a German immigrant and a Native American. When she married George Myers, her German relatives did not approve—they did not want her to be married to a black man. Her family disowned her, which created a heavy strain on their marriage. After they divorced, Florence left their two daughters with George, who then married Mary Dolly Green. George and Mary Myers had four children together, including Walter. After Mary Myers's death, Dean offered to take her daughters to live with her in New York. She felt that now she was financially able to take care of her girls.

Dean arrived in West Virginia with her new husband, Herbert Dean, who was also African American. The Deans were not wealthy, but they were much better off than the Myers family. Herbert Dean, happy to be a father to the two girls, also longed for a son. When he saw Walter, he was touched. Dean wanted a chance to raise him, to give him the stability and care that he needed. Walter was a sweet child, but at three years old, he was more than his exhausted father could handle. The Deans took Geraldine and Viola back to New York with them, and then a few months later, they sent for Walter. George Myers and Florence and Herbert Dean had talked it over and decided that Walter would have a better life with the Deans, who became his unofficial foster parents.

The Deans lived in a small apartment on 126th Street in Harlem. This predominantly African-American neighborhood of Manhattan in New York City has a rich history in African-American culture and art. Walter quickly adapted to life with his foster parents and thought of them as his real parents. Herbert and Florence gave Walter and his sisters much love and attention.

Herbert Dean worked as a handyman and shipping clerk for the U.S. Radium Corporation in downtown New York City. He also picked up extra work as a longshoreman, loading and unloading cargo at a local shipyard. It was not unusual for him to work two or three jobs at once. He even had a job working for the moving company owned by infamous gangster Dutch Schultz. When Walter was older, Dean worked as a janitor. Working hard and providing for his family were very important to Dean.

While Herbert Dean worked and the girls attended school, young Walter stayed home with Florence Dean. Sometimes she worked as a housekeeper, and later, she took a job at a button factory. When she was working, Walter stayed with a neighbor. Those early days, when it was just him and his foster mother, left a lasting impression on Walter Myers. He developed a close bond with her. Not only was she kind and patient, but she was also a good listener. Walter had no memories of his biological mother because he had been so young when she died. Even though he wished he could have known her, he always thought of Florence Dean as his real mother.

During those afternoons, Walter followed Dean from room to room while she cleaned and talked. They also listened to soap operas on the radio together. His foster mother liked to tell him German folktales and stories about blues singer Bessie Smith and child actor Shirley Temple. Once she even demonstrated a unique skill: yodeling. She read him stories from her favorite magazine, *True Romance*. Dean could not read very well herself, but she did introduce Myers to the act of reading. Soon he could pick out words on his own, and by age four, he could read. He recalled, "I didn't want to learn to read so much as I

TROUBLE WITH WORDS

wanted to be like Mama. I liked words and talking, and I wanted to be able to look at magazines and tell her the stories as she did for me."[2]

Though his foster father never read to him, Herbert Dean told Walter many stories. The grandson of a slave, Dean had grown up in Baltimore, Maryland, and he had stopped going to school in third grade. Instead of going to school, he went to work. Although he could not read very well, he was a fabulous storyteller. With Walter sitting on his knee, Dean would tell scary stories about monsters and other imaginary creatures. He changed his voice for the different characters and used funny and scary facial expressions. Walter loved to hear him tell stories, which always seemed believable, no matter how fantastic.

One time, Dean told Walter that a giant bunny rabbit was on the prowl, looking for children. Dean pretended that the rabbit was getting closer and closer, saying that the rabbit was walking toward their apartment building, and now climbing up the fire escape. Then suddenly Dean looked toward the window—the giant rabbit was right there, outside the window! Dean jumped up, and Walter followed him. They both ran down the street, yelling their heads off.

His mother's reading and his father's storytelling influenced young Walter Myers and were important in his path to becoming a writer. Walter also heard stories from Herbert Dean's father, a very religious man, who told Walter stories about the wrath of God.

When Walter was six, the family moved to a fourth-floor apartment on Morningside Avenue, right across from Central Park. Storytelling and lively talk filled the Dean household, and the radio was usually tuned into Big Band performers such as Cab Calloway, Duke Ellington, and Glenn Miller. On Sundays, the family attended church and strolled down Seventh Avenue in their good clothes. For Sunday school, the teachers stopped by to pick up the children, and they would walk down the streets in pairs, holding hands. Walter loved the colors and vibrancy of Harlem, and he especially loved the music that always seemed to be playing. He felt very much at home in the neighborhood: "Compared to Martinsburg [in West Virginia] I found Harlem a marvel, an exotic land with an inexhaustible supply of delights and surprise. . . . I loved Harlem and my new parents. The tarred streets, the fire escapes upon which we sought relief from the heat, two-sewer stickball, Chinese handball; this was the stuff of dreams."[3]

Harlem felt like a safe place, where the neighbors knew each other and helped each other out. Though the Dean family did not have much money, Walter never realized this—he always had food to eat and was never cold during the winter.

The first school that Myers attended was Public School (P.S.) 125 on LaSalle Street. He felt excited to start school—he already knew how to read and was looking forward to learning more. The first day did not go well, however, which set the tone for the rest of Myers's schooling. He realized he did not fit in with the other kids because of the way he talked.

Myers had trouble pronouncing many words, and when he spoke, his words came out sounding rushed and jumbled. His family could usually make out what he was saying, but everyone else had trouble. People around the neighborhood would offer him money just to hear him talk. The teachers could not understand him, and the other kids made fun of

TROUBLE WITH WORDS

him. The speech therapists could not figure out the trouble. Once he was even incorrectly diagnosed as having a hearing problem and fitted with a hearing aid. Because of his speech impediment, it is likely that Walter would have been placed in Special Education classes if he had not been such a good reader. Walter could already read on a second-grade level when he started school. The teachers could see that he was obviously a bright student.

Throughout elementary school, Walter was teased relentlessly. The kids called him Mushmouth. Walter felt embarrassed and angry. Big for his age, Walter was not afraid to fight back. His explosive temper and quick fists often landed him in the principal's office or in the back of the classroom. Once, when Walter was in second grade, a boy teased him, and Walter retaliated by hitting his tormenter. Walter was sent to the principal's office, where he was made to write "I will never, never hit any student in Public School 125" 500 times as a punishment. His parents told him he needed to learn to control his temper. Sometimes they gave him whippings as punishment, but it didn't seem to do any good.

Because Walter Myers felt humiliated, he lashed out at the other kids and the teachers. He also had trouble concentrating in school and, today, probably would have been considered hyperactive. The teachers believed they could not control him. The situation worsened until it reached the point where the school administrators considered expelling him. The last straw occurred in the fourth grade, after Walter and another student got into a physical fight. When the teacher yelled at him, Walter, frustrated, threw a book in her direction. The startled teacher moved and the corner of the book hit her shoulder.

In fifth grade, Myers started going to P.S. 43, a New York City public school in Harlem. It was there that he first encountered Mrs. Conway. She was rumored to be the meanest teacher in the school, but she was also the first person to give him a book that he liked.

TROUBLE WITH WORDS

This incident probably would have led to his expulsion if he hadn't been experiencing terrible stomach pains that day. His mother took him to the hospital, where he was diagnosed with appendicitis. The doctors immediately removed his appendix before it ruptured. To recover, Walter spent several weeks at home in bed. His mother and sisters spoiled him, bringing him food and drinks on a tray. By the time he could go back to school, it was time for summer vacation. The next year, for fifth grade, he enrolled in a different school, P.S. 43. His fifth-grade teacher was Mrs. Conway, who was rumored to be the meanest teacher in the school.

Did you know...

Walter Dean Myers's youngest son, Christopher Myers, is a writer and illustrator, and a Caldecott Honor and Coretta Scott King Honor recipient. He worked with his father on the picture books *Harlem*, *Blues Journey*, and *Jazz*. He also illustrated several of his father's young adult books. *Black Cat*, a book that Christopher wrote and illustrated himself, was named a Coretta Scott King Honor book. When Christopher was a child, his favorite pastime was drawing, and his parents encouraged him to practice every day for an hour and a half. Christopher continues to illustrate children's books. He is also a fine artist, photographer, and clothing designer.

One day, Walter Myers was again sent home for fighting in class. Mrs. Conway ordered him to sit in the back of the room and wait for his mother to pick him up. While he waited, he pulled out a comic book to read. He loved comic books. One of his neighbors, an older boy, threw them out when he finished reading them. Before the trash collectors came by to pick up the discarded comic books, Walter would carry them home. He accumulated probably 200 comic books this way. As he was reading and waiting for his mother in the back of the classroom, someone snatched the comic book from his hands. Startled, Walter looked up and saw Mrs. Conway tearing the book into shreds. She called him a "bad boy." He never forgot that moment.

The next week, Mrs. Conway brought in a stack of her own books for Walter and told him that he might as well read something good if he was going to read. One of the books was a collection of Norwegian folk tales, *East o' the Sun, West o' the Moon*. The book taught him about a faraway place and people. It was like nothing he had ever read before: "I realized I liked books, and I liked reading."[4]

Reading offered Walter an escape from his problems and from school. Throughout his childhood and adolescence, Walter could often be found at the George Bruce branch of the New York Public Library on 125th Street. In an interview, he explained, "Books took me, not so much to foreign lands and fanciful adventures, but to a place within myself that I have been exploring ever since. The public library was my most treasured place. I couldn't believe my luck in discovering that what I enjoyed most—reading—was free."[5]

TROUBLE WITH WORDS

Above is the George Bruce branch of the New York Public Library, located on 125th Street. As a child, Myers would take refuge in the library, later calling it his "most treasured place."

As a boy, some of Walter's favorite books were *Tom Sawyer, Little Men, The Three Musketeers,* and *Robin Hood.* Myers recalls: "I also felt a kind of comfort with books that I did not experience when I was away from them. I was, at times, almost desperate to fill up the spaces of my life. Books filled those spaces for me."[6]

One day Mrs. Conway suggested that the students write something of their own to read aloud. She had noticed that Walter had trouble pronouncing certain words and thought it might help him to let him read his own writing. Walter was good at communicating when he wrote down his thoughts, so he was excited about the assignment. He went home and wrote several poems that did not use any words that gave him trouble. Those were usually words that started with *w, u,* or *r* or that had the *ch* or *sh* sound in the middle. The next day, Walter read one of his poems aloud to the class, and everyone understood him. The kids did not make fun of him. Instead, they were impressed. At age 10, Walter started filling up notebooks with poems and stories.

When Walter wasn't reading or writing, he was usually playing with the other kids in the neighborhood. Harlem was an exciting neighborhood, "a magical place, alive with music that spilled onto the busy streets from tenement windows and full of colors and smells that made my heart beat faster."[7] Harlem was the home of many famous African Americans. Sometimes, Walter saw celebrated boxer Sugar Ray Robinson driving around the neighborhood in his lavender Cadillac. He also spotted Joe Louis, the heavyweight champion of the world, strolling down 125th Street. One time, poet Langston Hughes chased Walter's brother for a block because he had thrown a candy wrapper in Hughes's

The Church of the Master, located in Harlem, hosted many community events for area residents. Myers spent a lot of time there, between taking a modern dance class and playing basketball in the church gym. The church was torn down in 2008 because it was structurally unsound.

tiny patch of lawn. It was a vibrant, colorful world that would always stay with Myers.

A tall and muscular boy, Myers enjoyed sports almost as much as books. He loved the Brooklyn Dodgers baseball team and followed them passionately. With the other boys in the neighborhood, he played basketball in the church gym, handball against the church walls, and baseball at the sandlots on Morningside Drive. By the time he was 12, he was nearly six feet tall and physically aggressive—he made a good athlete. Sports weren't his only form of entertainment, however. He also attended plays at Teacher's College and took part in a modern dance class at the Church of the Master, a Presbyterian church on the corner of 122nd Street and Manhattan Avenue.

The Church of the Master served as a center for both religious and cultural events for the Harlem community. Later, it became the home for the Dance Theater of Harlem. When Myers was young, Josephine Baker, an African-American dancer, singer, and actress famous for her performances in Paris, put on a show at the church. It was also where Myers and his friends played basketball. The church basement gym had low ceilings that caused Myers and his friends to shoot "flat jumpshots." Later, Myers used this memory for the gym in his novel *Hoops*. The church was a big part of Myers's childhood memories. Not everything about it constituted a pleasant memory, though. Once he had to whitewash the walls of the church when the minister caught him throwing orange peels on the sidewalk.

When Walter entered sixth grade, his teacher was Mr. Lasher, an ex-Marine who had fought in World War II. By then, Walter had earned a reputation for being difficult to control. Mr. Lasher, Walter's first male teacher, quickly observed Walter's intelligence and creativity. He gave Myers both the confidence and guidance he needed to do better in school. He also arranged for Walter to have speech therapy. Walter went to the sessions but continued to experience trouble when he talked. Myers's childhood left strong impressions on him, memories that he would later write about in his books.

After doing well in middle school, Walter Myers went on to Stuyvesant High School, which was at the time an all-boys school. Stuyvesant, established in 1904, is a public school that requires students to take an entrance exam. The school focuses particularly on math and science, which were not Walter's strongest subjects. Above, students examine equipment in the school's laboratory in the 1950s.

3

Dropping Out

GROWING UP BROUGHT many changes. One change happened early. When Walter was in the fifth grade, his biological father moved to Harlem, bringing with him his new wife and children. Walter did not remember much about his father. Even though they now lived in the same neighborhood, their relationship remained very distant. Walter had little contact with his father, but he often saw his brothers and sisters and grew close to his brother George.

On Myers's twelfth birthday, his uncle, Herbert Dean's brother, was killed. The sudden death left Dean feeling very sad. He turned to religion and, for a while, distanced himself from his family. As Walter grew older, he felt that his relationship with his parents was becoming more strained.

Walter also began to feel uncomfortable about his love for reading. He often felt like he didn't fit in because he was such a bookworm. People in the community sometimes commented on how he always had a book under his arm. He began to take a brown paper bag with him to the library. This way he could hide the books that he checked out, so that the other kids wouldn't tease him. Walter knew that the other kids thought that reading wasn't cool.

It was easy for Walter to be alone with a book, but he also longed for friendship. He felt that reading set him apart: "What I had to hide was the self who was a reader, who loved poetry."[8] Even though he hid this part of himself from many of his friends, he never stopped reading. He recalls, "When I wasn't playing basketball, I read everything I could get my hands on."[9]

Several of Walter's teachers encouraged him along the way. His ninth-grade literature teacher, Mrs. Finely, liked to read poetry aloud to the students. She introduced Walter to the British poets, including Elizabeth Barrett Browning, who wrote *The Portuguese Sonnets*. Myers liked Browning's work. He also read Shakespeare, Coleridge, and Tennyson.

Walter read many books by English and white authors, but very few books by African-American authors. The teachers rarely assigned books by African-American authors, and Walter never encountered characters like himself or his friends. He didn't read about any

African-American kids growing up in Harlem. It might have been helpful, and inspiring, for Walter to find more positive, realistic images of African Americans in the books he read. Though he lived in Harlem, Walter was only somewhat aware of the Harlem Renaissance, which was not talked about much in his classes. During this important period, which began in the 1920s and lasted through the 1940s, African-American art, literature, music, and culture took the country by storm. The Renaissance was led mainly by the African-American community based in Harlem. Walter did not even know the work of its famous authors, such as Langston Hughes, Zora Neale Hurston, and Countee Cullen, until much later in his life.

As he grew up, Walter became more aware of racism. He noticed how the newspapers only talked about the accomplishments of white men who were usually politicians, doctors, and lawyers. He noticed how most of the people in Harlem worked as laborers or cleaning people. He began to wonder what this meant for him. What kind of future would he have? What kind of job could he get? He also encountered racism firsthand in his social circle. Throughout junior high, his closest friend was Eric Leonhardt, a German American. The Leonhardts owned a bakery on Amsterdam Avenue, in Morningside Heights, the neighborhood next to Harlem. The boys' mothers were friends, and Walter and Eric became friends in fourth grade. In junior high, things began to change, however. Girls expressed interest in blond, blue-eyed Eric, but not in Walter. Then, Walter found out that Eric was going to parties that Walter was not invited to because he was black. This made things tense between them. Later, in high school, they gradually drifted apart. It was a difficult realization for Myers: "Racism existed as a backdrop to our relationship, and I did not want to experience the humiliation of being rejected because I was black."[10]

Walter Myers's best performance in school was in junior high. As a restless, somewhat aggressive kid who ran around with troublemakers, he still managed to focus on his grades. His teachers recommended him for an accelerated program for junior high students, and he completed the seventh and eighth grade in just one year. Then his teachers recommended that he go to an all-boy's high school, Stuyvesant High School, one of the best schools in Manhattan.

Did you know...

In 1985, the first book in Myers's Arrow series was published. Ken and Chris Arrow are white teenagers who travel with their anthropologist mother, Carla, as she studies family life in various parts of the world: Peru, Hong Kong, Spain, and Morocco. Each story follows a typical structure. There is a stolen object and unexplained events; in the end, the clever boys always outsmart the villains. The books move at a fast pace and are from 83 to 90 page long. The titles include *Adventure in Granada, The Hidden Shrine, Duel in the Desert,* and *Ambush in the Amazon.*

DROPPING OUT

Stuyvesant High School, located in Manhattan, is a highly competitive school that focuses on math and science. These subjects were not Walter's strong points. He struggled with the classes and began to feel disenchanted with school. He also worried about his speech problem. Although his words sounded clear to him, others had trouble understanding him. He spent most of his free time reading, playing basketball, and hanging out with his friends. He began to lose confidence in himself. He did not know where he could go from here. What would the future bring? Would he be able to go to college?

Walter looked around and saw how few opportunities existed for African Americans. This was the 1950s. Many colleges in the United States were segregated, which meant they were for whites only. Walter wondered whether his family could afford to send him to college, even if he was accepted into an integrated college in the North. Could he possibly win a scholarship? There were very few scholarships available. Walter saw how hard his parents worked, and how little money they earned. It was difficult enough for them to keep him fed and clothed. How could they afford to pay for a college education?

Discouraged by his options, at age 15, Walter stopped going to school. He spent his days alone—reading, writing poems, and watching movies at the famous Apollo Theater on 125th Street. He also filled up his time thinking. He thought about race. He thought about the purpose of school. He wondered whether there was a God. Could he ever be a writer? What would the future bring? Why did people eat meat? For a while, he was a vegetarian.

He missed three weeks of school, sneaking the letters of truancy (letters saying that he had too many unexcused absences) from the school out of the mailbox before his mother could read them. Then he would forge letters by his mother to the school. Eventually, he decided to return on his own. He still didn't have any answers to his questions.

Walter felt like he didn't have any interests, except sports and reading. Blue-collar jobs, like the one his father had, did not interest him. He wanted to be a writer, which his parents couldn't understand. Though his father loved storytelling, he did not believe that a grown man could make a living from telling stories. He wanted Walter to be able to get a good job and to earn a living by working. In his 2001 memoir, *Bad Boy*, Myers explains: "While I had moved more into writing, and into reading, I was moving further and further away from my parents."[11]

Although Walter's father did not understand why his son always had his nose in a book, he still supported him, in his own way. More than anything, Walter wanted a typewriter. He had romantic dreams of becoming a writer, and imagined himself writing stories on a portable typewriter. He worked after school for a while in New York City's Garment District, saving up his pay. When he went to store to buy the typewriter of his dreams, he soon realized he did not have nearly enough money. When his father saw how disappointed his son was, he brought home a typewriter. Walter had his heart set on a portable typewriter, but his father gave him an old, beat-up Royal office typewriter instead. At first, Walter refused to use it. One day, however, he began

DROPPING OUT

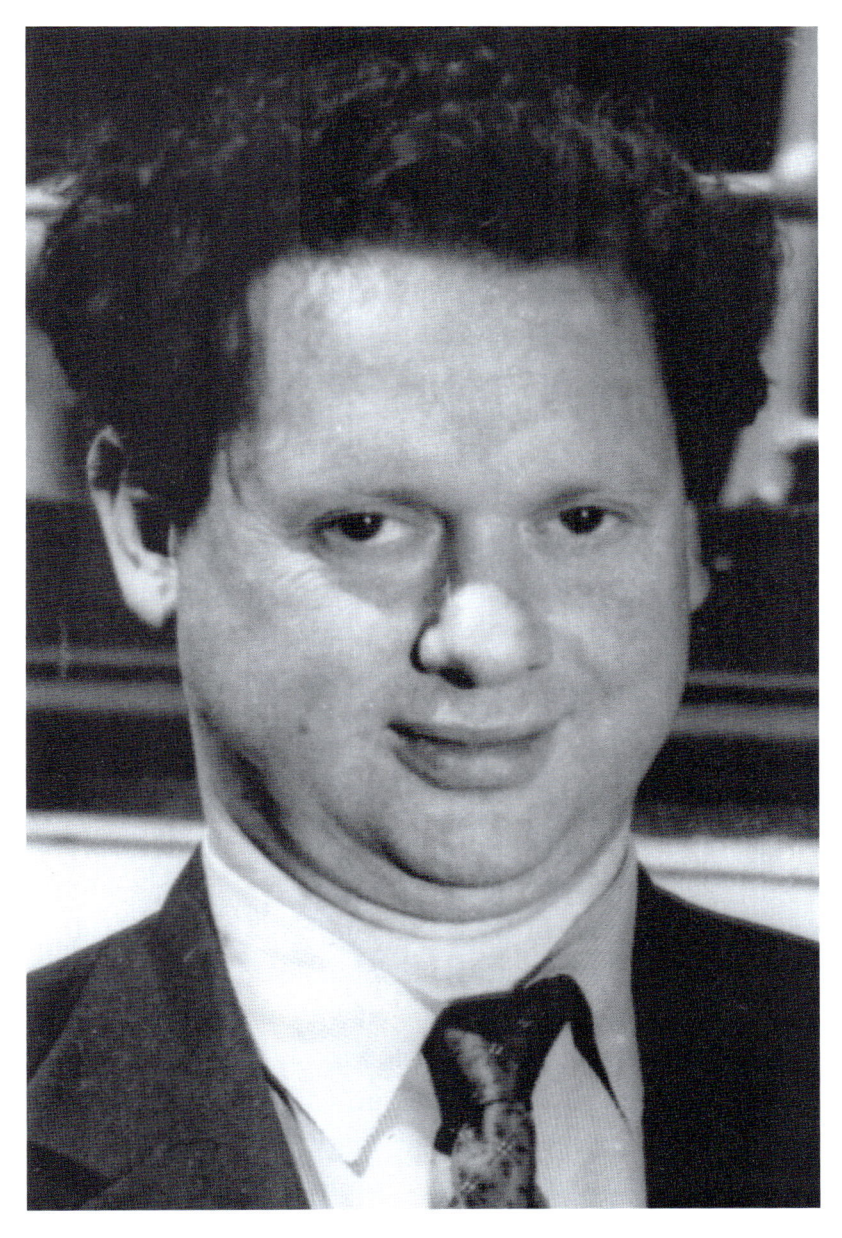

While in high school, Walter began writing and reading poetry. One of his favorite poets was Dylan Thomas. Thomas, pictured above, was a Welsh poet who often traveled to the United States, especially New York, on speaking tours.

typing on it and realized it would do just fine. Walter used the typewriter for the next 10 years.

Although Walter did not have much faith in school, good teachers continued to have an impact on his life. Mrs. Liebow, an English teacher, told Walter he was a gifted writer and gave him a list of important books to read, including *Penguin Island* by Anatole France, *Buddenbrooks* by Thomas Mann, and *The Stranger* by Albert Camus. Walter dove into the list. One particular writer who influenced him was Honoré de Balzac. Balzac was a nineteenth-century French author who is generally regarded as one of the founders of Realism in European literature. Walter read Balzac's fiction and realized that he wanted to be able to write the same kind of character-driven books. With Mrs. Liebow's encouragement, Walter entered writing contests. He won an essay-writing competition sponsored by *Life* magazine and, for the prize, received a year's subscription to the magazine.

Walter also continued to write poems. One of his favorite poets was Dylan Thomas. He had heard Thomas reading his poems on the radio and felt drawn to his deep Welsh voice. Walter knew that Thomas liked to hang out at the White Horse, a bar in Greenwich Village. A few times, Walter sneaked in to listen to the poet read. Walter was tall for his age and blended in, but when the bartender realized how young he was, he threw him out.

Walter's adolescence was somewhat troubled, and without reading, he may have been lost, like many of his friends. His most disturbed friend was Frank Hall, who had committed murder when he was a young boy and then spent time in a mental institution. Walter

DROPPING OUT

thought that Hall seemed mild mannered, but also very lost and directionless. Once, Walter helped protect Hall from three gang members, who wanted to beat him up. Another time, gang members chased Walter, but he slipped away by running up the stairs to a rooftop, then across the rooftop to a building on the corner. Later, he wrote about this in *Motown and Didi: A Love Story*. Walter never belonged to a gang, but for a while, he carried a knife—an Italian stiletto—for protection.

Walter spent less and less time at school. After he missed nearly 30 days, his mother found out. She would not let her son become a dropout. She took the train with him to school. She met with the guidance counselor, and while they were talking, Walter sat alone in the waiting room. Mrs. Liebow came by and asked if he was in trouble. He said he thought he was. She told him, "Whatever happens, don't stop writing."[12] The school gave him a break—he could come back, but he was placed under the supervision of a city agency for his truancy and had to report to a caseworker.

Walter entered his senior year of high school with anxiety. Writing seemed like the only thing he liked. What else could he do? He felt as though he had very little direction and few opportunities. He realized that, unless a miracle happened, he would not be going to college. His parents thought he was not being practical—they wanted him to grow up and get a job. He didn't know what to do with his life, but "what I did know was that I wanted to get away from anyone in the world who might care to ask me what I would be doing with my life."[13]

How could he be a writer? He didn't see any adults in his neighborhood who were writers. It did not seem like a possibility. The majority of authors that he read, and his heroes, were white. He felt invisible. Once, the woman he reported to at the city agency asked him if he liked being black. He was shocked by the question. He was even more shocked that he did not know how to answer her. "Being black had become, at best, the absence of being white," recalls Myers. "The clearest thing I knew was that there was no advantage to being black."[14]

During this time, Walter turned to poetry to find solace among the confusion. He read the war poems of Rupert Brooke, a poet who fought in World War I. The poem "The Soldier" had a particularly strong impact on Walter. Some of the more famous lines from the poem read:

If I should die, think only this of me:
That there's some corner of a foreign field
That is for ever England . . .

The idea of a dying on a battlefield, in a land far away, seemed almost romantic to Walter.

When Myers finally decided to go back to school, the building was locked: School was out for the summer. Myers felt terrible. He didn't know what to do. He made his decision after he walked past an army recruiting station on his way home—it seemed like the only way out. On his seventeenth birthday, August 12, 1954, Myers signed up for the U.S. Army. He joined the same year that the decision of *Brown v. Board of Education* ended school segregation. He waited to tell his parents until the day he was scheduled to leave. They were shocked. Why would he do this? His mother burst into tears. Herbert

DROPPING OUT

Dean did not understand his son's decision but gave him his blessing. Walter said good-bye and embarked on his journey.

The Cage is a basketball court on the corner of West 4th Street and 6th Avenue in New York City. When he lived in Manhattan as an adult, Myers would play basketball there to keep in shape. The Cage today is an extremely popular and competitive place to play street basketball.

4

A Children's Story

MYERS WAS SENT to Fort Dix, New Jersey, for boot camp, and after 16 weeks of basic training, he was stationed in Monmouth, New Jersey. He spent three years in the army. The United States was not at war during this time, so Myers mostly stayed on domestic soil playing basketball on the base and learning to repair radios.

During his time in the army, he was sent to the Arctic Circle, where the army had military bases. The Arctic is in the most northern part of the Northern Hemisphere, the area surrounding the North Pole. The landscape was like nothing Myers had ever experienced before—the snow was endless, and the ice creaked under his feet. He saw polar bears and the ice caps. The setting made a strong impression on him. Many years later, his memories would find their way into his writing. While he was in the army, Myers received news that his biological father had died. Myers mourned the loss of his father, although he had not known him very well.

When Myers was discharged from the army, he was 20 years old, and he still didn't know what he was going to do with his life. He was facing almost the same dilemma he had avoided during his senior year at Stuyvesant. With no other options, Myers moved back in with his parents and took a job at a factory. Florence and Herbert Dean had left Harlem and were now living in Morristown, New Jersey. Myers felt uncomfortable living in the suburban neighborhood and under his parents' roof. For three years, he had been on his own, and he did not want to give up his freedom and independence. He also missed the excitement of New York City.

During the days, Myers worked at the factory, a job he hated, and at night, he wrote. His parents did not understand why he wanted to spend all of his free time writing. Both of his parents had always worked with their hands, and it was hard for them to understand how writing could actually be considered work.

Myers thought he would move back to Harlem, but Harlem was not the same place—drugs and gangs were taking over. Instead, he rented a room in the rundown Cort Hotel on 48th Street in Manhattan. At the time, the area around the hotel was also rough. Myers had very little money and called this his "starving artist" period—he dropped nearly 50 pounds and fed himself on two dollars a day.

A CHILDREN'S STORY

Although Myers ate little, he devoured books as though they were food, reading as much as he could. For a while, he took a break from writing, but one day he set up his typewriter and his passion returned. He wrote poems, short stories, and articles. Once he started, it was as if he could not stop. During this time, he read "Sonny's Blues," a short story by African-American writer James Baldwin. The story left a strong impression on Myers. It was one of the first stories he'd read about the black urban experience. It helped Myers realize that he could write about his personal experiences and about the lives of his family, friends, and community.

Unfortunately, writing did not pay the bills. He sent his work out to magazines and received many rejection slips. To earn a living, Myers took on a variety of jobs. Then a friend suggested that he try getting a job with the U.S. Postal Service. Myers took the civil service exam and passed. He started working at the Post Office in 1959. That was where he met Joyce Smith.

After dating for a while, Walter Myers and Joyce Smith got married and soon expanded their family. Their daughter Karen was born in 1961, and their son Michael Dean was born two years later. During this time, Myers juggled work, writing, and taking care of his family.

After reading an ad in the *New York Post*, Myers signed up to take a writing class at a community college. Though Myers was intimidated at first, it was an important step. His teacher encouraged him to stick with writing, and Myers began to feel more like a writer. He left the class, though, after he realized he was writing more to impress the other students instead of writing what he wanted to write. He wanted to listen to his inner voice, to hear the stories he wanted to tell.

To stay active, Myers also played a lot of basketball, often at the court on Sixth Avenue in Greenwich Village known as the Cage. For a while, he played on a city basketball team called the Jolly Brown Giants. He also taught himself the flute and practiced constantly. Sometimes he would play a song more than 100 times, until he got it right.

Because work took up most of his time, Myers was not happy. Eventually, he was fired from the Post Office. He then took a job at the New York State Department of Labor. Myers began drifting away from his responsibilities at home and socializing with artists in the East Village. Trying to live the bohemian lifestyle, he played bongos at night clubs and learned the guitar and saxophone. He began drinking and spent more time hanging out with friends than with his family. His wife demanded that he change his behavior.

The apartment was getting too cramped for their family, so they moved to a house in Queens. Even though they enjoyed the extra space, the house put more financial strain on both of them. Myers and Joyce worked extra jobs to earn money. Their marriage felt distant and tense and would eventually end in divorce in 1970.

Using the G.I. Bill, a military education benefit that Myers earned because of his service in the army, Myers enrolled in classes at the City College of New York. He did not feel committed to school, however. He did not do well in his classes. He passed French, but failed English. During this time, he also began working with a therapist for his speech impediment. He heard about someone with a stutter who had finally lost it by speaking in a different accent. Myers tried this, and it worked. He especially liked talking with a Southern accent. This technique, plus the speech therapy, helped Myers to overcome his speech problem.

Myers kept writing at night, the only time he didn't have to be at work and wasn't busy with his children. He was now sending out articles to all kinds of magazines. He even wrote for the *National Enquirer,* a tabloid magazine. He wrote sports articles covering bullfighting and kickboxing that were published in men's magazines such as *Blue Book*, *Argosy*, and *Cavalier*. He also began writing poems and adult adventure stories. His work appeared in many magazines for blacks, including *Black World, Black Creation,* the *Liberator*, and *Negro Digest.*

Myers was writing during the height of the Black Arts Movement, part of the Black Power Movement. The Black Arts Movement was founded in Harlem by the writer and activist Amiri Baraka (formerly known as LeRoi Jones). It encouraged African-American writers to use vernacular dialogue and to emphasize black culture and politics. It was an arts movement that went hand in hand with political activism.

In 1968, Myers heard about a contest for the Council on Interracial Books for Children. This organization demanded that the publishing industry publish more material by black authors. They were offering an award for black writers of children's books. Myers decided to give it a try. Little did he know that this contest would change his life.

Myers won $500 for *Where Does the Day Go?* and the story was published as a picture book by *Parents' Magazine*. Critics praised the book for portraying a positive relationship between a black father and his son and for depicting children from several different ethnic backgrounds. This was Myers's first published book. When he was 33 years old, Myers enrolled in a writing workshop at Columbia University taught by the writer-in-residence, African-American novelist John O. Killens. Killens had founded the Harlem Writers Guild, an organization that encouraged and supported many black writers and artists. He was a good influence on Myers. When Killens heard about an editing job at Bobbs-Merrill Publishing Company, he encouraged Myers to apply. Myers was doubtful. He had no editing experience and did not even have his high-school diploma. The publishing company was impressed by Myers and hired him as an acquisitions editor. This meant that Myers helped decide which manuscripts the company published. One of the first manuscripts that he helped publish was a book of prose called *Gemini*, by the African-American poet Nikki Giovanni.

Monday through Friday, Myers went to work at the office at 57th Street and Fifth Avenue. He had never dreamed that he would be in this position. How did a high-school dropout become an important editor, with a large office and a secretary?

Myers worked full-time and spent as much time as he could with his children. His marriage had ended in 1970. Though Joyce Myers had full custody of the children, Walter Myers made sure he was still a big part of their lives. Myers also continued to write articles and short fiction for magazines and signed a contract with Bobbs-Merrill to write a nonfiction book.

In writing *Where Does the Day Go?* Myers realized that he enjoyed writing books for children. His second picture book, called *The Dancers*, was published in 1972. *The Dancers* is about a young African-American boy named Michael who befriends a white ballerina. Fascinated with ballet, Michael invites the ballerina to his house. She dances for Michael and his friends, and then Michael and his friends teach her one of their dances, the Funky Chicken.

A CHILDREN'S STORY

The book received good reviews. Parents and librarians felt that the strong father-son relationship in the book sent a positive message to kids. They also liked that Myers had written about ballet in a way that included a male audience. The book won a Child Study Association of America's Children's Books of the Year citation.

With the publication of his second book, Myers made the important decision to change his name from Walter Milton Myers to Walter Dean Myers, in order to honor his foster parents. He was pleased that his mother had the chance to see the bound book, with his new name on it, before her death. Florence Dean died of heart disease in 1972. It was a sad day for Myers. He would miss the patient woman who used to read to him from her *True Romance* magazines. Although their relationship had grown more distant during Myers's adolescence, they still had a strong bond between them and loved each other very much.

Myers's third picture book was called *The Dragon Takes a Wife*. In this book, Myers took a traditional fairy tale and

Did you know...

The Young Landlords was made into a movie in 1983. Myers did not work on the script for the film, and he was not happy with the movie. In 1997, *Tales of a Dead King* was made into a Hallmark made-for-TV film called *Legend of the Lost Tomb*, starring Stacy Keach. Recently, Whoopi Goldberg acquired exclusive rights to make a film of *At Her Majesty's Request*.

retold it in a modern way. The setting is the inner city, and the dragon, Harry, gets the advice of Mabel Mae Jones, a black, street-smart fairy, who says things like "What's bugging you, baby?" or "I can get down with that." Myers was surprised by the controversy the book stirred up. Some parents complained that Myers was ruining a traditional European fairy tale. Others complained that he was stereotyping African Americans. Still others complained about the use of street slang. Myers thought he was writing in an honest and humorous way. This was Myers's first taste of controversy and censorship, but it would follow him over the course of his career.

Myers met Constance Brendel a few years before this, when he was still working at the New York State Department of Labor, where Brendel also worked. Soon, the two married. Their son, Christopher, was born in 1974.

While Myers was working at Bobbs-Merrill and learning more about the publishing world, he decided to get an agent—someone who could sell his writing to publishers. His agent gave one of Myers's short stories to an editor at Viking Press. The editor mistakenly thought it was the first chapter of a novel. When she ran into Myers at a party, she told him how much she liked the first chapter. She wanted to know what happened next. Myers quickly made up a plot. The editor was impressed and offered Myers a contract to write the novel.

Fast Sam, Cool Clyde, and Stuff, Myers's first novel geared toward teenagers, was published in 1975. The publication of this book meant a lot to Myers: "It changed my life because I had no real education, and I needed something to validate myself. I needed to find value, and publishing gave me that value."[15]

The novel received good reviews, including one by the young adult author Robert Lipsyte, author of *The Contender*. Lipsyte wrote, "Walter Dean Myers has a gentle and humorous touch, especially with dialogue."[16] The novel won the Woodward Park School Annual Book Award and was selected as an American Library Association (ALA) Notable Book. The ALA is the oldest and largest library association in the world. Each year, it provides a list of recommendations for the best books published that year.

Children, parents, and teachers hoped to hear from Myers again. He had written a few picture books and one young adult novel: What would he publish next?

Myers now knew that he wanted to write books for teenagers. He wanted to write more books like *Fast Sam*, books that portrayed African-American kids in a realistic way, the kind of books that were not available when he was a boy.

Just when it seemed like everything was falling into place, his life suddenly took a sharp, unexpected turn. Like many companies during the time, Bobbs-Merrill decided to make cuts in order to survive the unstable economy and Myers was laid off. At the age of 40, he was unsure about what to do next and how to care for his family. He decided to go on the trip to Hong Kong, Bangkok, and Thailand that he had already planned. His wife and son Michael went with him. While they were traveling, Myers and his wife discussed their options. Where would Myers go from here? Writing was Myers's real passion, but he was not sure that he could make a living as a writer. Finally, they decided that he should at least give it a try. It was a scary but exciting decision: Myers would not look for another day job. He was leaving the comfort of a full-time job, with regular pay and heath benefits, to be a writer. Would he be able to make it?

Deciding to become a full-time writer did not come easily to Walter Dean Myers. He had a family to take care of, which included son Christopher (right), shown here with Myers in 1999.

5

Full-Time Writer

AFTER MYERS DECIDED that he would try to be a full-time writer, he knew that he needed to treat it like a full-time job. To be a full-time writer, he would need to write, of course. He would also need to work out ideas, outline books, and conduct research. Myers figured out a schedule. He set a goal to write 10 pages per day. A disciplined writer, Myers felt confident about this plan. Still, he was nervous. Would he have enough ideas? Would he write enough books? Would he make any money?

These questions were soon answered. Within a year of deciding to write full time, Myers's *Mojo and the Russians* was published, followed in the next two years by *It Ain't All for Nothin'* and *The Young Landlords*. All three books, which are set in Harlem, received positive reviews. *Mojo and the Russians* is rather comical and playful in tone, whereas *It Ain't All For Nothin'*, which earned an ALA Notable Book citation, is more serious. *It Ain't All For Nothin'* focuses on Tippy, a boy who must chose between the values of his father, who lives a life of petty crimes, or his God-fearing grandmother. The book portrays the pressures of being young and black and growing up in Harlem.

The Young Landlords also focuses on the experience of young African Americans living in Harlem. A group of devoted friends try to make their neighborhood a better place to live. They purchase a dilapidated building on West 122nd Street, becoming landlords, and face the tremendous responsibilities of dealing with their eccentric tenants. *The Young Landlords* received mostly positive reviews, though *Kirkus Reviews* commented that "the whole thing is a little hard to credit." The reviewer points out that if "it's all a little goody-goody, Myers as usual cloaks his straight-and-narrow messages in easy colloquial dialogue and street-corner savvy."[17] For this book, Myers won the prestigious Coretta Scott King Award. This award, sponsored by the ALA, was created in honor of civil rights leader Dr. Martin Luther King Jr. and his wife, Coretta Scott King. The award honors Martin Luther King's work of fostering peace and unity and Coretta King's work to support social justice.

In general, critics praised Myers for creating well-developed, complex characters instead of relying on easy stereotypes. Some of the characters were based on his childhood friends; others he modeled after his children. He explained that Stuff (from *Fast Sam, Cool Clyde, and Stuff*) and Tippy were based "to some extent on the character and personality of my son, who is quite sensitive and given to moments of great tenderness. Writing about him allowed me to escape the stereotype of the tough, street-smart, old-before-his-time Black kid as offered as typical."[18]

The 1980s brought many changes to Myers's life. His daughter Karen attended Queens College but then left school to get married. She had a son in 1981—Myers's first grandson. Myers's oldest son, Michael, in his last year of high school, was trying to figure out what to do with his life, and Christopher had entered elementary school. Myers's kids weren't the only ones in school. Myers enrolled at Empire State College in a program that gave credits for life experiences. He took a variety of classes, from photography to criminal justice. For a criminal justice class, he spent hours interviewing prisoners, defense attorneys, prosecutors, and juvenile delinquents. He then organized the data and wrote a 600-page paper. He graduated in a year, earning his B.A. in communications.

Myers also volunteered to teach composition and writing at a Jersey City middle school. He taught sixth, seventh, and eighth graders twice a month; they called themselves the "Creative Spirit of P.S. 40." Myers gave the students interesting assignments such as interviewing their elders. One of his star pupils published a short story in *Shoe Tree,* a children's magazine. Myers also devoted time to coaching Christopher's Little League baseball team.

There were more ideas, more books, and more awards. The variety of Myers's books impressed critics. Although he is best know for his novels that take place in Harlem, starting in the 1980s, he also began to write adventure tales, leaving the familiar urban setting for more exotic places.

The Golden Serpent, a mystery-fable directed toward young readers, is set in India at the beginning of the twentieth century. The book tells the story of a wise man who is summoned by the king to solve a mystery. For older readers, Myers wrote *The Legend of Tarik*, which takes

WALTER DEAN MYERS

FROM THE AUTHOR OF *MONSTER*, WINNER OF THE PRINTZ AWARD

Walter Dean Myers

Lonnie was talking about stealing again . . .

It Ain't All For Nothin'

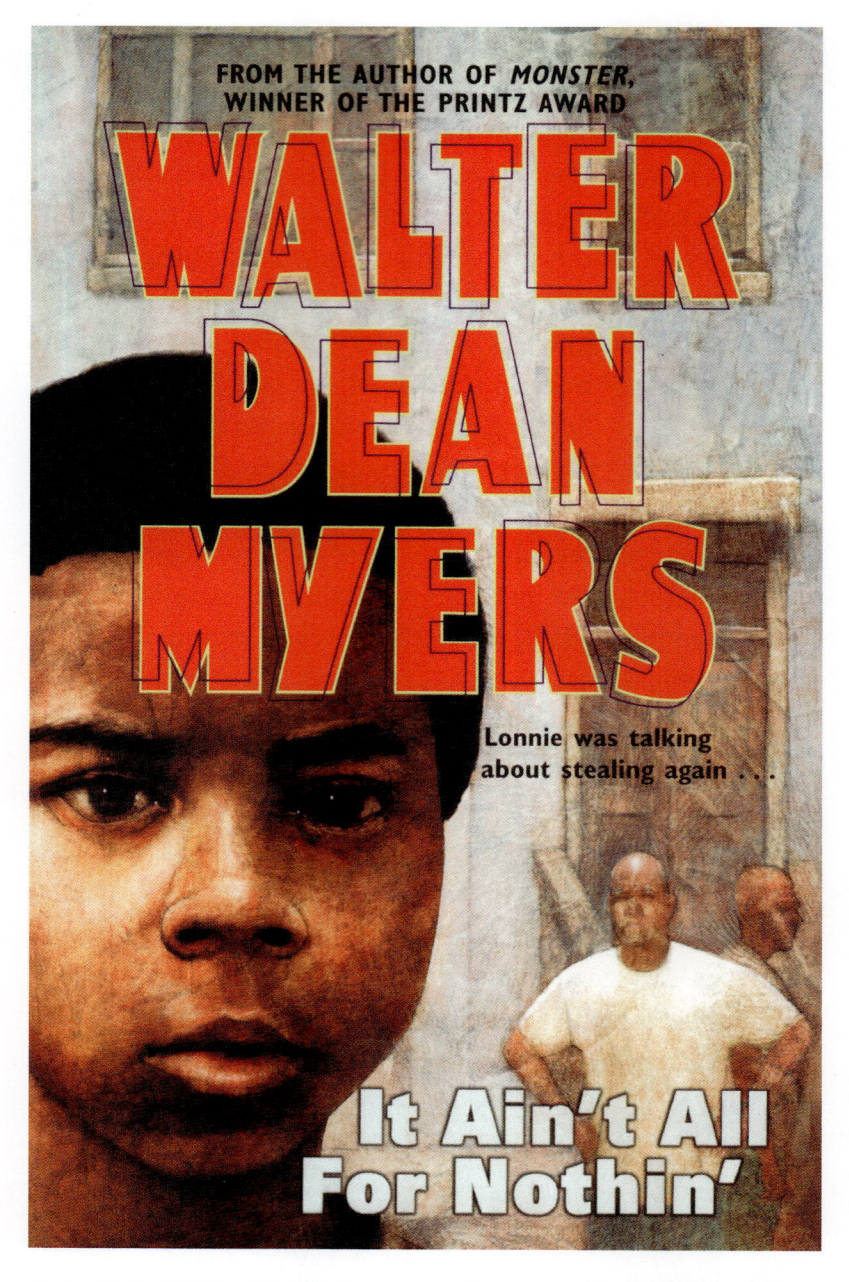

In *It Ain't All For Nothin'*, *a young boy must choose between his father's lifestyle of petty crime and his God-fearing grandmother's values. It explores many of the pressures young people face growing up in Harlem.*

place in Morocco, and *The Nicholas Factor*, which is set in Peru. These adventure books, very different from books like *It Ain't All for Nothing*, were set in faraway places. *The Legend of Tarik* earned Myers a Notable Children's Trade Book in the Social Studies citation and an ALA Best Book for Young Adults award. This book follows Tarik, a young black hero, who battles the evil El Muerte and in the end makes the decision to live in peace.

Myers also wrote *Tales of a Dead King*, an exotic thriller set in Aswan, Egypt. In this book, for the first time in Myers's work, the main characters were white. Before this, all the main characters in Myers's books were African American. Myers continued in this direction with the Arrow series, a set of adventure novels starring two white teenagers, Chris and Ken Arrow.

Although Myers enjoyed writing the adventure books, he did not abandon writing realistic novels about African American teenagers growing up in Harlem. In the 1980s, Myers published several important books, including *Hoops*, *Won't Know Till I Get There*, *Motown and Didi: A Love Story*, and *The Outside Shot*.

Hoops, one of several of Myers's books about basketball, tells the story of 17-year-old Lonnie Jackson, who is about to graduate from high school. Lonnie faces a major dilemma when he and his coach are offered large sums of money to shave points off a game. Lonnie must reach his own understanding of right and wrong and, in the end, learns hard lessons about life. *Hoops* earned critical acclaim and was selected for an ALA Best Book for Young Adults. *The Outside Shot* was the sequel to *Hoops* and follows Lonnie to college.

Won't Know Till I Get There follows in the style of *Fast Sam*: it deals with serious issues but for the most part relies on light humor. The novel focuses on 14-year-olds Stephen Perry and Earl Goins, a troubled streetwise kid whom Stephen's parents are considering adopting. After the boys are apprehended for spray-painting graffiti on a subway car, a judge orders them to do community service at an old-age home. The novel won the Parents' Choice Award for its examination of foster parenting and for the portrayal of the cross-generational relationships between teens and the elderly.

Motown and Didi: A Love Story, one of Myers's early realistic novels, earned Myers a second Coretta Scott King Award. For the first time in his young adult fiction, Myers abandoned the use of the first-person point of view and instead used the third-person point of view to tell the stories of Motown and Didi. Motown, who lives on his own but was once a foster child, struggles to survive in an environment filled with temptation and danger. Didi dreams of

Did you know...

At the end of the 1990s, Myers published three fictionalized works that were part of the My Name Is America series. These were *The Journal of Scott Pendleton Collins: a World War II Soldier; The Journal of Biddy Owens: The Negro Leagues;* and *The Journal of Joshua Loper: a Black Cowboy.* The My Name Is America series, published by Scholastic, features stories that are part-fact, part-fiction and are told through the eyes of young boys from ages 12 through 16. The stories show children what it was like to grow up in a different era of American history.

leaving, but must deal with her drug-addict brother, who dies of a drug overdose, and her mother, who has a nervous breakdown. Frustrated by the endless struggles, Didi just wants to get out of Harlem: "It was hard, life in Harlem, and Didi couldn't take it. It was too much for her."[19] Motown and Didi both rely on their inner strength and their support of each other.

In the decade after Myers made the decision to become a full-time writer, he published many books. His realistic novels about teens growing up in Harlem achieved popular and critical acclaim. He also wrote adventure stories, ghost stories, and picture books, including *Mr. Monkey and the Gotcha Bird*. The idea for this book came from a story that Myers had told his restless young son Michael when they were on a 22-hour flight to Hong Kong, years ago. Myers also published an interactive book for Teachers & Writers Collaborative (a nonprofit organization that publishes teaching materials) called *Sweet Illusions*. The book focuses on teen pregnancy and abortion. At the end of each chapter are blank pages for students to write down their thoughts and responses. *Sweet Illusions* was used in many schools to help students discuss the topic of teen pregnancy.

Everything seemed to be going well for Myers and his family. Then, in 1986, Myers's foster father died. Sick with cancer, Herbert Dean died in a veteran's hospital. Overcome with grief, Myers began researching his family origins and submerged himself in his writing. During this time, Myers learned that his father was illiterate. Myers had always assumed that his father could not read very well, but when he was going through some of his father's papers, he realized that his father had barely known how to read or write at all. This discovery helped Myers understand why his father did not want his son to be a writer and why he had not read any of his son's books.

When Myers and his wife started to look for a new place to live, they came across buildings in New York City that cost as little as $25, but would cost many times that to restore to a livable condition. The deteriorating buildings above, in 1980s Harlem, may have looked like the abandoned buildings that inspired Myers to write **The Young Landlords**.

Endless Ideas

MYERS HAS PUBLISHED over 80 books. Where does he get all of his ideas? Is he ever afraid that he will run out? Myers is a curious, observant, and adventurous person. His ideas for his books come from memories and personal experiences, but he also likes learning about places and people that are unfamiliar to him. The ideas for his books have come from a variety of sources, so he never seems to be short on possibilities.

Myers frequently turns his life experiences into stories. For example, in 1978, he and his wife decided that they needed a bigger apartment. When they began house hunting, they came across buildings in New York City that were for sale for as little as $25. The buildings were falling apart: They had leaky roofs, broken windows, and missing plumbing. Because fixing up one of those buildings would cost too much, Walter and Connie Myers ended up buying a house in Jersey City, New Jersey, where they still live today. The idea of the abandoned buildings stayed with Myers, and he started thinking about the situation and wondering what would happen if some teenagers bought one of those buildings. This idea led to *The Young Landlords*.

Myers also draws inspiration from things that upset him. "Whatever bothers me becomes an idea for a book. Example: bullying. I see that so much so often. I go to juvenile detention centers and I see the young people in juvenile detention centers, so I write about those kids. Whatever I see inspires me."[20]

Traveling in so many parts of the world has also given Myers many ideas. He loves learning about different lands and cultures and has been to many interesting places around the globe. He started traveling in the mid 1970s, when he went on a trip with his older son, Michael, to England, France, and Italy. Soon after, he went to Greece with his wife and younger son, Christopher. In the 1970s, he traveled to South America, Egypt, and Peru, where he and his family camped in a rain forest on the Amazon River. Myers had gone to the area to acquire information for an article that he was writing on bullfighting, but while he was there, he also found important material for *The Nicholas Factor*, his spy thriller about the natives of Iquitos on the Columbia-Peru border. Myers often travels to do research for his books. For example, for *Tales of a*

Dead King, he visited Aswan, Egypt. One of his favorite research projects was the traveling he did for *The Legend of Tarik*. He told Scholastic, "I enjoyed doing the research on that book. I went to Spain and North Africa. I liked writing the story."[21]

Other personal experiences also shape Myers's fiction. He sometimes bases a book on an incident from his life or on people he has known. For example, *Me, Mop, and the Moondance Kid* was based on Myers's experiences with Christopher's Little League baseball team. Similarly, when Myers wrote his critically acclaimed *Fallen Angels*, he was thinking about his younger brother, who was killed in Vietnam.

Myers wrote *Fallen Angels* as a tribute to Sonny, one of his younger brothers from Martinsburg. Years before, when Myers visited home while in the army, he was wearing his uniform, which left an impression on his younger brother. Sonny followed in Myers's footsteps and joined the army. By the time Sonny joined, however, the United States was at war with Vietnam. The Vietnam War was a military conflict in the 1960s and early 1970s. American soldiers were sent to Vietnam to fight against the spread of communism. The war lasted more than 10 years. It was very unpopular with the American public. American troops were finally withdrawn in 1973, after thousands of American and Vietnamese lives were lost.

Sonny died in Vietnam on May 7, 1968, only two days after he arrived. The loss of his brother deeply affected Myers's views toward war. Once Myers took a trip with his son Chris to the Vietnam Veterans Memorial in Washington, D.C., to make a rubbing of Sonny's name, one of the 58,249 names inscribed on the wall. He mourned his

WALTER DEAN MYERS

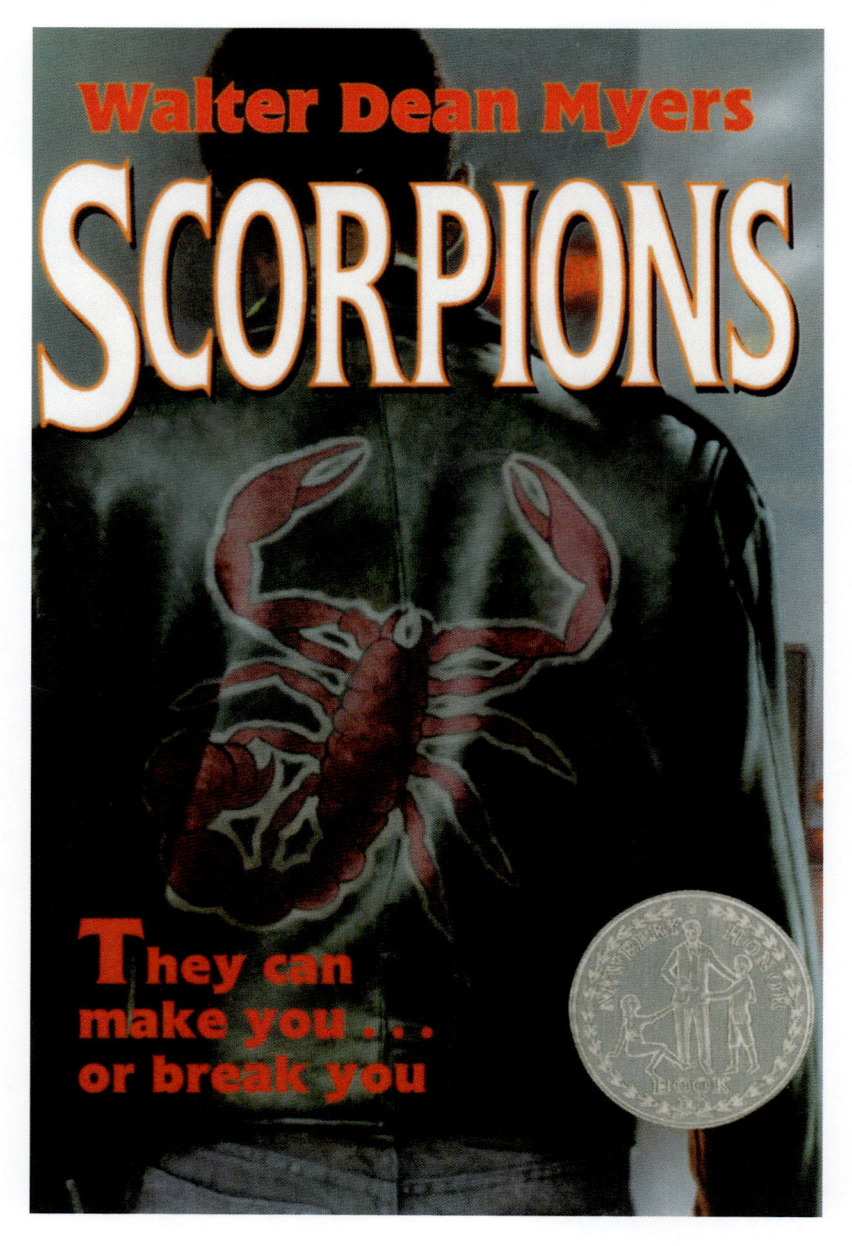

Myers wrote Scorpions in the 1980s, during a time when many major American cities were experiencing a crack epidemic. In the novel, 12-year-old Jamal Hicks feels pressured to take over the Scorpions when his older brother, the former gang's leader, is sent to prison.

brother's death and wrote an essay for *Essence* magazine on the guilt he felt for setting such an example for his brother. It took nearly 20 years for him to be able to write *Fallen Angels*.

The novel is about Richard Perry, an African-American solider who wants to get out of Harlem. College is not an option, so he joins the army, thinking he'll at least be given meals and a place to sleep. He quickly discovers the horrors of war. The novel, told through the eyes of Perry, is both about the Vietnam War and about Perry's coming of age. Most critics praised the book. In the *New York Times*, Mel Watkins wrote, "'Fallen Angels' is a candid young adult novel that engages the Vietnam experience squarely. It deals with violence and death as well as compassion and love, with deception and hypocrisy as well as honesty and virtue. It is a tale that is as thought provoking as it is entertaining, touching, and, on occasion, humorous."[22]

A realistic, dramatic novel, *Fallen Angels* won the ALA Best Book for Young Adults, the Parents' Choice Award, and the Coretta Scott King Award.

Like many of his books, Myers did extensive research for the book. His book was a tribute to his brother, but the characters were based on the many different people that Myers met when he was researching the novel. To develop the story, Myers researched historic firefights from the National Archives, consulted the Vietnam Veterans Outreach Center, and interviewed war heroes and the survivors of soldiers killed in combat. He also traveled cross-country by Amtrak and visited the hometowns of his fictional cast.

The same year that *Fallen Angels* was published (1988), Myers also published *Scorpions*, one of his best-known books. This book was inspired both by personal experience and by what Myers observed: "I was writing here about a scene I know only too well, about a family like so many I grew up with—low-income families, headed by a single parent, a hard-working woman who leaves her young children every morning and carries around with her all day long a fear that they may go wrong."[23]

When Myers wrote *Scorpions* in the 1980s, New York and many other U.S. cities were struggling with the presence of crack cocaine, as well as with guns and gangs. African-American communities were being torn apart by the drugs, violence, and prison sentences. The Harlem setting in *Scorpions* is much rougher, and the tone is less optimistic, than in earlier books that Myers had set in Harlem.

Did you know...

At a used book shop in London, the owner handed Myers a packet of letters that would lead to Myers writing a book. These letters concerned a young West African princess who was rescued from death by a British captain, an opponent to slavery. Renamed Sarah Forbes Bonetta, the girl returned to England where she met Queen Victoria, who took an interest in her and provided her with an education. These letters inspired Myers to write *At Her Majesty's Request: An African Princess in Victorian England* (1999).

ENDLESS IDEAS

The Harlem that 12-year-old Jamal Hicks lives in is overrun with crack, crime, and gangs. His older brother, Randy, is leader of a gang called the Scorpions and is in jail for murder. Jamal feels pressured to take over as the gang leader. Though he does not want to be a part of the violence, he sees how easy it would be to make money by running crack. Jamal is also intrigued by the respect he gains after he obtains a gun from another gang member. His life changes when he accepts the gun.

A local shooting also pushed Myers to start writing *Scorpions*. He and his son Christopher used to play basketball in the park. At one point, one of the kids they played with regularly stopped showing up, without any explanation. Later, Myers found out why: "I thought he had just lost his interest in the game, but then I read that he had shot someone. This bothered me quite a bit, and when something bothers me, I write about it. The issue, in my mind, was the kid having a gun. That's why I gave Jamal the gun in the book."[24]

Myers thought it was important to address the proliferation of guns—how easy they were to get, and how they were ruining lives. He understood that things are much harder for young people today than they were in his day. He explains:

> When you're young, you make mistakes. The big thing that's different now is that when I was a kid, you could survive your mistakes. Then, if you got into a gang fight, you hit someone with a stick or you threw a bottle . . . today kids have access to guns. The same kids that would have been in trouble and gotten a stern talking-to are now going to jail for fifteen or twenty years. Instead of having a bloody nose, you're dead.[25]

With *Scorpions,* Myers was writing about a subject that was rarely discussed in young adult literature but that needed to be addressed. The book impressed critics. For example, *Kirkus Reviews* said, "Myers uses street rhythms and language to tell his story in a tough, honest fashion, making clear that such tragic events have many causes. . . . A painful story with a conclusion that offers escape as an answer—but not as a solution."[26] *Scorpions* earned an ALA Best Book for Young Adults and was selected as a Newbery Honor Book.

With the publication of *Scorpions*, Myers began to receive many letters from confused and lonely teenagers. They felt that Myers understood their problems and that he was writing about their world in a realistic way. They sometimes wrote asking Myers for advice. Many kids from the inner cities had never seen their lives portrayed in a book before. Myers's books were reaching an audience that was often ignored or misunderstood. Myers explains:

> I think that sometimes people don't understand the differences in the lives of children from the inner city. Perhaps that child hasn't had breakfast that morning and perhaps that child doesn't have a quiet place to do homework. And perhaps that child doesn't have someone waiting for them at home. Yet the child is not going to say to a teacher, "I'm hungry" or "I have no one at home." So the child puts on an act of bravado. The child says something to the effect of "I don't care." This is something you hear all the time from children: "I don't care." And of course they care. They all care. But they have to put on this defensive act that, "I'm a tough guy. I'm tough. I don't care."[27]

Although the story line of *Scorpions* is tragic, Myers wanted to send a hopeful message to kids with his book. He says, "When I write about Jamal, I'm trying in my books to show disadvantaged kids how important it is to value themselves."[28]

In Myers's critically acclaimed book Monster, *the 16-year-old protagonist is on trial for a crime he may not have committed. When Myers first conceived of the story, it was in the form of a play. His editor suggested he try it as a book.*

7

Teens in Harlem

ALTHOUGH MYERS WRITES many different kinds of books, he is best known for his realistic young adult novels. These novels, usually set in Harlem, portray African-American teenagers who are growing up in a harsh environment and must deal with very real problems, such as overcoming the temptations of drugs and gangs, as in *Scorpions*, or holding together families that are torn apart by crime and poverty, as in *Somewhere in the Darkness*.

Myers's realistic urban novels tackle contemporary issues, including racism, drugs, death, and sex. There are usually moments of violence and loneliness, and the characters often find they must make difficult choices, as with Lonnie Jackson, Motown and Didi, or Jamal Hicks. Myers is trying to break down barriers and reach young people through his complex characters and realistic stories. Despite the bleak situations, Myers's message is positive: Young people must believe in themselves and persevere.

Several themes show up regularly in Myers's work. Often, he writes about African-American fathers and sons and what happens when the father is not around. He has also written about fostered or orphaned children. Friendship is also an important theme in his work. In many of his books, the protagonist, a young African-American male, finds help by developing a friendship with an older, wiser person, as with Motown and the Professor. In the prologue to *Handbook for Boys*, Myers explains how important it is for young people to have mentors: "I particularly love the idea of mentors, especially in those areas where there are not a lot of successful role models."[29] Myers shows again and again how the characters survive, despite the dangerous influences and temptations around them.

Myers has only written a few books with female protagonists. For example, Didi, in *Motown and Didi*, is a strong young woman who deals with her mother's mental breakdown and her brother's drug addiction. In *Crystal*, an early Myers novel, the main character is on her way to becoming a top model, but she must figure out if she is willing to compromises her values for the job.

Myers believes it is important to write about African-American children and to give them role models and characters they can identify with. In an essay that was published in the *New York Times*, he recalls how, as a child, he rarely encountered black characters: "The overwhelming *absence* of blacks in most books were telling the children of my generation that being black was not to be taken seriously."[30] White characters were the only role models for African-American children. Myers has worked hard to convince the publishing world to publish more books about the African-American experience, while also encouraging teachers and parents to support these books.

Tired of seeing African-American characters portrayed as stereotypes, Myers tries to create complex characters in his work. He does not want his characters to seem perfect. His characters, whether black or white, have weaknesses and flaws and make mistakes. He wants his characters to resemble real people. He says:

> Stereotyping of young Black people is not just a literary problem, it's a social problem as well. If teachers can find in my books a way to convey the notion that there is a common humanity among all of us I will be satisfied. Not all Black kids are athletes, or tough, anymore than they are pickpockets or vandals. Some, like Stuff, like my son, are complicated, funny, unsophisticated, not very street-smart kids just trying to find out who they are, as we all are.[31]

Myers also includes characters from other ethnic backgrounds in his work. For example, in *The Beast* Gabi is Dominican. Sometimes the novels show both the tension and the potential friendships between African-American and white characters. For example, in *Me, Mop, and the Moondance Kid*, Myers portrays a close friendship among two young African-American boys and a white girl. In *Slam!* the main character has trouble adjusting to the mostly white magnet school he attends. Similarly, Spoon, the main character of *The Beast*, finds himself out of his element at a rich school in Connecticut.

When Myers entered the writing scene in the 1970s, he was something of a pioneer. In the 1960s, juvenile publishers published very few books with African-American characters. Some of the books about African-American characters in the early 1970s were written by white authors and often lacked authenticity. According to the critic Rudine Sims Bishop, "By 1975, when *Fast Sam* was published, Myers saw himself as part of a new beginning."[32] Bishop points out that Myers began publishing just when other important African-American writers were also making contributions to young adult literature. For the first time, publishers were printing books that depicted realistic, complex portrayals of young African Americans living in American cities. Some of these books included June Jordan's *His Own Where*; Alice Childress's *A Hero Ain't Nothin' But a Sandwich*; and Kristin Hunter's *The Soul Brothers and Sister Lou*. "Myers's contribution in his early books was to add a much needed touch of humor to the developing portrait of Black life in the city. . . . Myers called attention to the laughter that is also a strong tradition and one of the tools for survival," attests Bishop.[33]

Novels such as *Scorpions*, *Motown and Didi*, and *Monster* have touched many teenagers, reaching black and white audiences, and Myers's more recent books have also reached a large audience. Myers's mailbox regularly overflows with fan letters. Teenagers write to tell him how his books have helped them through difficult times. They feel connected to the characters' feelings of isolation and loneliness; they identify with the struggles and pressures the characters encounter. Many of the teenagers who read his books have experienced similar troubles, such as having a relative in prison.

Myers's books have also inspired many children to read, and his work reaches a part of the population that the majority of young adult books do not—young, urban, African-American males. He hopes that his books appeal to young bookworms, but he also wants to reach kids who don't normally spend time reading: "I write to give hope to those kids who are like the ones I knew—poor, troubled, treated indifferently by society, sometimes bolstered by family and many times not. I was a high-school dropout, and I know how easy it is for them to lose their brightness in a web of drugs, gangs, and crime."[34]

Did you know...

When Myers sent the manuscript *Monster* to HarperCollins editor Phoebe Yeh, it was in the form of a play. Yeh suggested that Myers reframe Steve's journal entries as a novel. Myers could use the journal to take readers through some of the scenes. Myers's son, Christopher, created the illustrations for the jacket and the 15 interior illustrations. A photographer took pictures of various subjects posing as characters in the book. Jackie Harper, from HarperCollins, posed as Steve's mother, and a brother of Chris's girlfriend posed as Steve. Chris used scans of these photographs to help create the final illustrations. The fingerprints are Myers's.

Myers's inspiration for Fallen Angels *was his younger brother, who died in Vietnam. Many young men in the late 1960s and early 1970s were sent overseas to participate in the conflict. The soldiers above carry a wounded comrade in November 1965.*

Critics praise Myers's work for his compassionate storytelling, sympathetic characters, and realistic dialogue. A few reviewers have criticized some of his books for uneven, undeveloped plots, but most of the reviews have been overwhelmingly positive.

Critics are often particularly enthusiastic about Myers's vivid characters. One of the most important points of writing fiction is writing believable characters. The characters lead Myers through his stories. Myers says that when he writes, "I know exactly what I want to say, I know exactly where I'm going with a book. The only things that change are the way the characters react. I think I know how a character will react, but that could change. Otherwise I know exactly where I'm going."[35]

Most of Myers's characters are inspired by real people, but they are not based exactly on one person. Most of them are composite characters. This means that he may base one character on one, two, or three people in real life. These can be strangers, friends, or family. He also develops a profile and history for each character. A character profile is like an in-depth résumé. It could list the character's hobbies, likes and dislikes, and family background. The character becomes like a real person. Myers even knows what his character looks like. After Myers sketches in the details for each character, he will look through his large collection of photographs, as well as some newspapers and magazines, for pictures of people he thinks resemble his characters. His wife Connie makes a collage out of all of these pictures, and Myers hangs it on the wall in his office to look at while he is writing.

Critics also highlight Myers's ear for natural-sounding dialogue. From the beginning of his writing career, Myers has felt comfortable using street slang and African-American vernacular in his work. Sometimes his characters use profanity. Teens appreciate the realistic language in his books. The characters in his books talk the way readers and their friends talk. Myers also often writes from the first-person point of view, and readers can quickly feel connected to the characters. "They recognize the environment. They're drawn to the books because they hear a language they are familiar with. They hear names and circumstances that are familiar things, so the book becomes a friendly place to be," Myers explains.[36]

Although Myers's books are popular with teens and critics and have won numerous awards and honors, they have also faced endless scrutiny and heated controversy. Many of Myers's books have been challenged and banned from schools, with parents and school boards complaining about profanity and violence. Myers defends his books as realistic. His novels reflect the real problems that teenagers are facing, and he lets his characters talk about those problems the way teenagers talk in real life.

Myers's first encounter with book banning occurred in 1983, when school administrators in Ohio challenged *Fast Sam*. In 1989, *Hoops* made the American Library Association list of banned books, after a Colorado district challenged the work. A year later, *Fallen Angels* appeared on the ALA banned book list when Ohio schools objected to the profanity. His children's books have also faced challenges. A school board member in Queens, New York, challenged *Young Martin's Promise* because of opposition to the political ideas of Martin Luther King Jr. The book, however, stayed on the library's shelf.

Beginning in 1982, the American Library Association has sponsored "Banned Books Week: Celebrating the Freedom to Read," which is observed during the last week of September each year. This event reminds Americans not to take for granted the precious democratic privileges of free speech and intellectual freedom. The week celebrates the freedom to choose or to express one's opinion, even if that opinion might be considered unpopular. The

ALA stresses that books must be made available to all who wish to read them.

During Banned Book week in 2000, Myers claimed seventh place on the ALA's list of the top 10 most censored authors for *Fallen Angels*. Other top authors whose books have been banned include Maya Angelou, Judy Blume, Stephen King, J.K. Rowling, Alice Walker, Robert Cormier, and Louis Lowry. In 2005, the ALA listed *Fallen Angels* at the top of the list of banned books, with objections to violence, offensive language, and racism.

Walter Dean Myers is shown here working at his home in New Jersey. Many of Myers's books have won critical acclaim and awards.

8

Critical Acclaim

THROUGHOUT THE 1990s, Walter Myers wrote prolifically and published a large number of books. His work includes a mix of realistic dramas, humorous novels, adventure and fantasy books, picture books, and nonfiction. Humorous novels included *The Mouse Rap*, while serious dramas included *Somewhere in the Darkness*, *The Glory Field*, and *Monster*. He also wrote *Shadow of the Red Moon*, which is both a fable and a fantasy story, and *The Righteous Revenge of Artemis Bonner*, a comic novel set in the frontier towns. In 1992, Myers started the 18 Pine Street series, the first mass-market series to star black characters, which include *The Test*, *Fashion by Tasha*,

Intensive Care, and *Dangerous Games*. Other published books included *Smiffy Blue: Ace Crime Detective: The Case of the Missing Ruby and Other Stories*; *Harlem Blues*; and a picture book, *How Mr. Monkey Saw the Whole World*.

Over the span of his career, Myers has won many awards and honors. He is a five-time winner of the Coretta Scott King Award for African-American authors, and he has also won the Newbery Honor Book award twice. In 1994, he received a tremendous honor when the Young Adult Library Services Association awarded him the Margaret A. Edwards Award. This is a lifetime achievement award given to recognize a body of work. Other authors who have won this prestigious award include S.E. Hinton, Richard Peck, Robert Cormier, Louis Duncan, and M.E. Kerr. The committee singled out *Hoops*, *Motown and Didi*, *Fallen Angels*, and *Scorpions*, praising Myers for writing stories that showed compassion for the urban teen.

In addition to fiction, Myers writes nonfiction for children and young adult readers. Many of these books are about African-American heroes and leaders. Myers wants to provide young readers with a sense of pride and understanding of their African-American heritage and history. These books stress black culture, community, and history, such as *Now Is Your Time! The African-American Struggle for Freedom*. This book, Myers's first contribution to black history, covers issues of race and human rights and focuses on the black experience in America. It also includes a historical account of his own biological family. Myers had been thinking often about his roots and where he came from. He researched his family history and relied on his sisters to help him with family history details. For *Now Is Your Time!* Myers won his fourth Coretta Scott King Award, an ALA Best Books for Young Adults and Notable Books for Children, and a

CRITICAL ACCLAIM

National Council of Teachers of English Orbis Pictus Award for Outstanding Nonfiction.

Myers's biographies on important African-American figures include *Young Martin's Promise*, a biography of Martin Luther King Jr. and *Malcolm X: By Any Means Necessary,* a young adult biography of Malcolm X. Like Myers's best fiction, his biographies depict well-developed, complex characters. He also wrote a picture book on the Haitian activist who led a rebellion against the French, *Toussaint L'Ouverture: The Fight for Haiti's Freedom*. The book is illustrated with paintings by the African-American artist Jacob Lawrence.

Myers is curious about historical events. He began reading and doing research about mutiny on the slave ship *La Amistad* in 1839, which led to the publication of *Amistad: A Long Road to Freedom*.

Myers also likes to go to junk shops, thrift stores, and flea markets, and sometimes he gets ideas from what others consider junk. He is a big collector of old things. Myers owns a collection of over 3,000 black history books and over 1,000 old photographs of African Americans. In fact, a photograph that Myers found led to one his most praised nonfiction books, *Brown Angels: An Album of Pictures and Verse*. This is a picture book that contains poems written by Myers, alongside found historical photographs of black children from the early 1900s. Myers was inspired to write the book after he found the first photograph at a flea market. The picture moved him and led him to finding many more. *Brown Angels* was selected as one of the New York Public Library Books for the Teen Age in 1994. A few years later, Myers published *Glorious Angels: An Album of Pictures and Verse*, another collection of antique photographs of African-American children.

Following this trend of photos and text, in 1996, Myers published *One More River to Cross: An African American Photograph Album*, with pictures of African Americans and text about what African Americans have endured over the course of history. The book sets black and white photos of ordinary people, alongside portraits of such famous African-American figures as Frederick Douglass, W.E.B. Du Bois, Billie Holiday, Marian Anderson, Jackie Robinson, and Booker T. Washington. Photographs are a good way to reach readers. The people in the pictures look back at you. You can study the photograph and then read the text and understand something significant about the person's life. Another one of Myers's photojournal books, *Angel to Angel: A Mother's Gift of Love*, begins with a poem that Myers wrote for his mother when he was 10 years old.

In 1997, Myers began an important collaboration with his son Christopher Myers. Christopher is an illustrator and artist. The father and son have worked together as a team on several books. The first book they did together was *Harlem: A Poem*, which was selected as a Coretta Scott King

Did you know...

Many of Walter Dean Myers's books have also been turned into audio books. These include

Bad Boy
Dream Bearer
Blues Journey
Blues of Flats Brown
Handbook for Boys
Monster
Shooter

CRITICAL ACCLAIM

Honor Book in the illustrator category and as a Caldecott Honor Book. Myers wrote the poems for the book, and Christopher illustrated, using paper cutouts, portraits, and ink and gouache in blues, gold, and browns. The book is a tribute to Harlem, its history, music, and dreams.

Myers also wrote several important, realistic novels during the 1990s. In the first part of the decade, he published *Somewhere in the Darkness*, which earned many awards. The novel focuses on a troubled father-son relationship. Cephus "Crab" Little, an ex-con, takes his son Jimmy out of Mama Jean's care to go on a cross-country journey. Like many of Myers's novels, there is no easy, happy ending. Refuting sentimentality, Myers captures the painfulness and heartache of adolescence.

Another important dramatic novel is *The Glory Field*, which Myers wrote most of at the MacDowell Colony. The MacDowell Colony is a residency in New Hampshire that provides writers and artists with room and board, along with peace and quiet. It is a good place for a writer to get a lot of work done. Myers won a fellowship and was able to write a lot while he was there.

The Glory Field received acclaimed reviews, with some critics comparing the book to Alex Haley's *Roots*, which was published in 1965. *The Glory Field* covers several generations of an African-American family, beginning with the enslavement of 11-year-old Muhammad Bilal, who was taken from Sierra Leone in 1713, to the Lewis family reunion, which takes place in 1994 on the family land in South Carolina. The novel covers important historical events, including the Civil War, the Depression, and the civil rights movement. It also chronicles the years of economic hardship that an African-American family faces in twentieth-century American society. In a positive review in the *New York Times*, Kenneth C. Davis praised the book but also said, "Such a big bite may be more than can be chewed in one book. The worthy effort proves perhaps too ambitious," and suggested that it could have been made into several separate books, so the reader has more time to get to know the various characters."[37]

With *Slam!* Myers returned to writing about one of his favorite sports. The award-winning *Slam!* follows 17-year-old Greg "Slam" Harris, who plays basketball for a mostly white magnet school. The novel is written in the first person, with Slam introducing himself to the reader: "Basketball is my thing. I can hoop. Case closed. I'm six four and I got the moves, the eye, and the heart."[38] Greg loves basketball, but not school. He struggles with his grades, and he is also worried about his sick grandmother. He is close to his mother and brother but feels disappointed in his father: "Me and Moms and Derek are like a real family; so is Pops when he's acting right, which means he's working. When he's working he's like laid back at home and he's mostly off the bottle."[39] The novel is set against a Harlem landscape of drugs and drive-by shootings. Greg is worried that his best friend Ice, also a ball player, may be dealing drugs. Like many of Myers's characters, Greg must make critical choices. Myers wrote this book after he had observed how so many young athletes were staking their futures on the slim chance of making it professionally. He was concerned how young athletes can be tempted and manipulated, yet he also wanted to show how basketball can give a young person self-confidence.

Myers ended the 1990s with one of his most powerful and critically acclaimed books, *Monster*. Sixteen-year-old Steve is on trial for murder and could face the death penalty. During the trial, Steve pictures all the events as if he were directing a movie; he decides to write a script about the experience. The script is interspersed with Steve's handwritten

CRITICAL ACCLAIM

journal entries that describe his emotions. The novel depicts the courtroom drama and a jailhouse setting, with flashbacks to the robbery that resulted in a shopkeeper's murder. The characters—defendants, witnesses, lawyers, and Steve—speak for themselves, and the reader is left with many questions: Did Steve serve as a lookout for their robbery? Was he in the store? Did he commit murder?

When Myers wrote this, he was thinking about how children can quickly lose their childhood in a single moment. He was also thinking about the political atmosphere, and how so many young black men were getting locked up for life. He explains:

> The other side of the "war on crime" is the huge number of young people caught up in the juvenile justice system. They're getting involved with drugs, gang fights, petty robberies, etc. More and more teenagers like Stephen are being tried as adults. Everyone writes and talks about stopping crime, I thought I needed to write about it from the teenagers' point of view.[40]

Myers wrote this book during a time when there was public outrage at the rise in juvenile crime. The research he did back in school, when he compiled 600 pages of prisoner interviews, helped him to construct the book. He also attended a seminar on criminal justice run by the New York City prosecutor's office and interviewed 25 inmates in prisons in New York and New Jersey.

Monster was the first winner of the Michael L. Printz Award. This is an award for a book that "exemplifies literary excellence in young adult literature." It is named for a Topeka, Kansas, school librarian who was a longtime active member of the Young Adult Library Services Association. The award is sponsored by *Booklist*, a publication of the American Library Association.

Walter Dean Myers is a disciplined writer. He sticks to a strict schedule and tries to write 5 to 7 pages each day.

9

Discipline, Dedication, and Fun

DOES MYERS EVER think about writing for adults again? He has considered it, but for him, writing for teenagers is both necessary and rewarding: "I think I write mostly for teenagers because my own teenage years were difficult years for me. I look at those years, and they were so difficult, and I had questions about what life was about. Even when I try to write for adults, I find myself switching to teenagers, to teenage points of view."[41]

Myers is drawn to writing about young people. He wants to capture their struggles, hopes, and dreams. He once explained,

"I'm drawn to the eternal promise of childhood, and for the flair of the young for capturing the essence of life."[42]

A year after the publication of *Monster*, Myers published *145th Street: Short Stories*. For these 10 short stories, Myers turned once again to Harlem. The Harlem in these stories is portrayed as a hopeful, magical place. It was 145th Street that inspired him to write these stories: "I like that street very much. I hang out on that street. I like the small shops and the people and I wanted to give them a voice. Some of the stories are actually true stories that I remembered from growing up in Harlem. I reproduced the entire neighborhood."[43]

Other recent novels that take place in Harlem are *Handbook for Boys: A Novel*, set around a barbershop on 145th Street, and *The Beast*, which follows 17-year-old Anthony "Spoon" Witherspoon. He leaves Harlem to attend Wallingford Academy in Connecticut, where he feels out of place among privileged preppies. When he returns home for Christmas break, he is upset by how Harlem is ravaged by drugs and alcohol and must rescue his Dominican poet girlfriend, Gabi, from her drug addiction. The voice in this book is different from many of Myers's other first-person perspectives. Spoon's voice is more sensitive and poetic. He wonders, "What were we going to do? Now that we were glimpsing our whole selves, our selves with blemishes and faults, with saints that sometimes failed us and beasts that sometimes brought us comforts, what were we going to do with these new selves?"[44]

Focusing on African-American heroes, Myers wrote *The Greatest: Muhammad Ali*, which documents the life of Muhammad Ali, from his childhood to his Olympic victory in 1960 to his life as professional boxer. Other nonfiction books include the *USS Constellation* and *Antarctica:*

DISCIPLINE, DEDICATION, AND FUN

Journeys to the South Pole. Myers also coauthored, with Bill Miles, the nonfiction book *The Harlem Hellfighters: When Pride Met Courage*, which tells the story of the 369th Infantry in World War I, a regiment composed entirely of African-American men, that was nicknamed the "Harlem Hellfighters." Myers also published another biography on Martin Luther King called *I've Seen the Promised Land: The Life of Dr. Martin Luther King, Jr.*

Myers published more picture books and poems. *Blues Journey* documents black music from slave call-and-response songs to the blues. This book is another father-son team effort. Christopher Myers illustrated the book with shades of mostly blues, browns, and whites; Myers wrote poems to capture the spirit of the music:

> *Blues, blues, blues*
> *sliding through the night*
> *Blues, blues, blues*
> *sliding through the night*
> *If you looking for a soft bed,*
> *I'll leave on the light.*[45]

Another book of poems is *Here in Harlem: Poems in Many Voices*, made up of 54 poems, each written in a separate voice that is modeled after the people Myers knew growing up.

Myers continues to write about difficult, potentially controversial subjects. One subject that he has written about several times is the negative effects of war. In addition to *Fallen Angels*, he published *A Place Called Heartbreak: A Story of Vietnam*, which describes the seven-year, four-month imprisonment in North Vietnam of Colonel Fred V. Cherry, the first black POW of the Vietnam War. More recently, he published a children's picture book on the Vietnam War called *Patrol*. This book tells the experience of a young soldier on his first patrol as he lies in wait for his enemy. In the *New York Times Book Review*, the reviewer says the book "at its core is a condemnation of warfare."[46] He added that if "'Patrol' has a shortcoming, it is that it may be an intellectual stretch for the youngest of Myers's readers to gasp the larger theme, to see that this is basically an antiwar essay."[47] Myers won the Jane Addams Award for *Patrol*. This award is given to a children's book that promotes peace, social justice, and equality. In his acceptance speech, Myers stated that he hoped kids saw the book as condemning the glorification of war. Not only had he lost a brother to war, Myers had also worried about his son Michael, a chaplain for the air force, when he served in the Persian Gulf War in 1991. Michael returned home safe and sound.

Myers's popular and critically acclaimed *Shooter* is not about war, but it is a novel about young people, guns, and violence. *Shooter* is about a high school shooting. The shooter, a student named Leonard, shows up at school one day with his guns and goes on a shooting spree, killing Brad, a jock who constantly bullied him, and then killing himself.

Myers felt driven to write this book after the shooting in Littleton, Colorado, that occurred on April 20, 1999. At Littleton's Columbine High School, 2 students killed 12 other students and one teacher and wounded 24 others before committing suicide. The massacre made headlines around the world and Columbine became a household name. Myers went looking for answers. He explains: "After the Columbine incident, I was upset. I went out to Colorado and spoke to some people out there. What I saw was kids being bullied, pushed around, sometimes by fellow students, sometimes by family members. These kids

DISCIPLINE, DEDICATION, AND FUN

would get so angry and upset. I saw kids being bullied, and I saw them reacting to being bullied."[48]

Told from multiple perspectives in the aftermath of the shooting, the reader learns about the shooter, Leonard, through in-depth interviews with his best friend, Cameron, and his ex-girlfriend, Carla. The interviews are conducted by a school psychologist, an FBI agent, a threat analysis specialist, and the town sheriff. The structure of the novel is made up of interviews, newspaper clippings, and the diary of Leonard. Over the course of the story, Myers reveals Leonard's angst and loneliness. *Shooter* received powerful reviews, including this one in the *New York Times Book Review*: "As in all his work, Myers himself evinces an honesty that challenges even as it captivates."[49]

Another one of Myers's more recent dramatic novels is *Autobiography of My Dead Brother*, which opens with a funeral for a 14-year-old killed in a drive-by shooting. This is a sobering story. The Harlem setting includes drive-by shootings, funerals for young black men, and drug dealing. Fifteen-year-old Jesse feels like he's losing his best friend, Rise, who has turned to dealing drugs. His search for the "old" Rise leads him to art. He begins to create a biography of Rise in pictures, using illustrations and comic-style panels. Christopher Myers helped out again with this book, providing his father with the illustrations.

Myers's work habits have not changed much since he decided to become a full-time writer. He still works at home in a small office. He produces about two books a year. How does he write so many books?

Myers learned early on that to be a successful full-time writer, he would have to be disciplined. Though he does not work a nine-to-five job at an office, he still follows a strict schedule. He has a certain routine. First, Myers wakes up every morning between 4:30 and 5:00 A.M. Some of his best ideas come early in the morning. Then he takes a five-mile walk around the neighborhood to loosen up and clear his

Did you know...

Fallen Angels was challenged many times in the twenty-first century. These incidents were reported during the Marshall University Libraries Banned Books Week, 2006:

2006   Removed from the Blue Valley School District's high school curriculum in Overland Park, Kansas.

2005   Challenged for racism, offensive language, and violence.

2004   Banned at the Franklin Central High School in Indianapolis, Indiana, because of concerns about the book's profanity.

2003   Challenged in Fairfax, Virginia, school libraries by a group called Parents Against Bad Books in Schools for "profanity and descriptions of drug abuse, sexually explicit conduct and torture." It was also banned from George County, Mississippi, schools for profanity.

2002   Banned for offensive language, racism, violence, and being unsuited to age group.

2001   Challenged, but retained in Arlington, Texas, junior high school libraries, despite a parent's complaint that the book's content was too strong for younger students.

DISCIPLINE, DEDICATION, AND FUN

head. He comes back around 7 A.M. and showers. He then sits at his desk and works.

When he first started his career as a full-time writer he tried to write 10 pages a day; now, because of so many projects, speaking engagements, and obligations, he tries to write between 5 and 7 pages per day. Myers believes that anyone can learn to write, but they need to be dedicated and practice. He explains: "What I earnestly believe is that writing can be learned by anyone truly interested in language and literature. The trick is not to wait for inspiration, but rather to train yourself to sit down and write on a regular basis. Writers don't fail because they don't write well, they fail because they don't produce."[50]

Sometimes people think of a writer just sitting down at a desk and writing a story in a single setting. Usually, writers go through many rewrites and revisions. Myers does not sit down and write the story from beginning to end. There are several steps that go into the creation of his books. First, he develops the outline for the story, which helps him figure out the plot. Much of the writing is actually the "prewriting." He explains: "I make a living by pre-writing. I'm a great pre-writer. I plan my stories. I plan very carefully. What I do, is I outline a story in six boxes. Six-part outlines. Expand it to scenes. I keep expanding the outline, until I see that I have a complete spectrum for a book. If it doesn't turn out, I destroy that idea. I outline every single book, every single story I write."[51]

Next, Myers writes the first draft very fast. Then, he rewrites, which takes more time and thought. In the rewrite, he works out problems. He might have to add more details and background information about a character, or fill out a scene, or tighten the plot.

Because Myers works on many different projects at once, it is important for him to keep a schedule, with deadlines and goals. He sets daily goals, such as finishing a chapter, and long-term goals, such as a set date to begin a new project. Staying organized helps Myers handle everything. Myers follows a schedule for his daily goals, but he also has a big, master schedule, with deadlines and goals for future projects.

Myers feels lucky that his favorite hobby is also his job. He says, "For a person with speech difficulties, writing was a way of communicating easily. It was my hobby more than a way of making a living. I'm surprised to actually be able to make money doing the thing I love."[52]

Myers's family has stuck by him over the years. His wife is a great source of support. She looks over Myers's manuscripts, and he also discusses ideas with her.

It is important for Myers to get feedback on his work before he is ready to send it to his agent. He likes to get the input of his wife, son Christopher, and sometimes other readers. When Myers finishes a book, he first gives it to his son to read. Next, his wife reads it. They write their comments, which Myers looks over. Sometimes Myers also hires teenagers to read the books, which he finds very helpful: "They tell me if they like it, or if they found it boring or interesting. They have very good comments to make. If I go to a school, I'll find teenagers. Sometimes kids write to me and ask me if they can read."[53]

Now that he has become such a popular writer, Myers finds himself much in demand. Over the years, he has taught writing classes and has had many speaking engagements around the country. Myers is a popular speaker, and his talks always bring in a big audience. He speaks at schools, libraries, bookstores, and conferences. He was

DISCIPLINE, DEDICATION, AND FUN

a keynote speaker at the annual Young Adult Literature Conference in 1994, and he also delivered the graduation address at Jersey City State College. In 2002, children from Detroit public schools chose Myers as the featured speaker for the city's fourteenth Author Day.

Myers enjoys talking to kids and hopes to inspire them to read and write. He is active in outreach programs. For example, he participated in the National Basketball Association Reach to Achieve program, to encourage a lifelong love of reading. It is his hope that his books can help kids with some of their problems: "I think that many of the problems I put into the books help kids engage problems intellectually before they confront them on the street."[54] Myers understands the power of a book, but he also recognizes the limitations: "I'm not interested in giving kids something that will all of a sudden change their lives. Just having kids think about it is important."[55]

Through his speeches, lectures, and essays, Myers challenges schools, teachers, libraries, and publishers to provide their young people with books that depict African-American experiences. He believes there needs to be more books geared toward African-American children, so that they have positive images of themselves and their neighborhoods. In his essay "I Actually Thought We Would Revolutionize the Industry," he warned parents that they needed to buy books about African Americans and children from other ethnic backgrounds. He continued this theme with "Telling Our Children the Stories of Their Lives," when he confronted publishers of fiction and textbooks for omitting African-American characters and experiences.

Myers still lives in Jersey City with his wife and often travels around the world to do research. With such a busy schedule, how does Myers unwind? He still finds time to have fun. He spends time with his grandchildren, plays the flute, does crossword puzzles, and watches basketball. His favorite team is the New York Knicks. His dream, if he weren't a writer, would be to be a professional basketball player.

If Myers had not been such a big reader when he was a kid, he probably never would have become a writer. Myers's advice to kids who like to write and who may want to be a professional writer one day is to "develop excellent reading habits. You have to be able to read to write. Every writer that I know reads a great deal. Second thing is discipline. . . . It's the combination of discipline and reading."[56]

As far as Myers is concerned, he will continue writing books for the rest of his life. He has made major contributions to young adult literature, providing a positive, authentic portrayal of African-American life in the United States, and created memorable characters. Myers wants young people to go after their dreams. He hopes they turn to books, not guns, and let their imaginations and creativity take them places. "As a last comment," he says, "reading good books opens the world to you. We all need to read more."[57]

CHRONOLOGY

1937 Walter Milton Myers born August 12 in Martinsburg, West Virginia.

1940 Myers's mother dies; Herbert and Florence Dean move to New York City and informally adopt Myers.

1954 Myers leaves Stuyvesant High School, joins U.S. Army, and serves three years.

1955 His biological father, George Myers, dies.

1957 Myers moves to Midtown Manhattan and works a variety of jobs.

1960 He marries Joyce Smith.

1961 His daughter Karen is born; Myers enrolls in a writing class.

1963 His son Michael Dean is born; Myers begins writing for African American and men's magazines.

1966 Myers begins working as vocational placement supervisor for New York State Employment Service, a job he held for three years.

1968 *Where Does the Day Go?* wins first prize in a writing contest sponsored by the Council on Interracial Books for Children.

1969 *Where Does the Day Go?* is published as a picture book by *Parents' Magazine* Press.

1970 Myers becomes editor at Bobbs-Merrill Company; Joyce and Walter Myers are divorced.

1971 Myers changes name to Walter Dean Myers.

1972 His foster mother, Florence Dean, dies.

1973 Myers marries Constance Brendel.

1974 His son Christopher is born.

1975 His first young adult novel, *Fast Sam, Cool Clyde, and Stuff*, is published.

1977 Myers decides to be a full-time writer.

1978 Myers and his family move to Jersey City.

1980 He receives Coretta Scott King Award for Fiction for *The Young Landlords*.

1984 Myers graduates in a year at Empire State College.
1985 He begins Arrow series.
1986 His foster father dies from cancer in veteran's hospital.
1988 Myers receives MacDowell Colony Fellowship.
1991 *Now Is Your Time! The African-American Struggle for Freedom* is published.
1992 Myers begins writing the 18 Pine Street series.
1993 *Malcolm X* is published.
1994 Myers receives the Margaret A. Edwards Award for lifetime achievement in writing for youth, with the committee singling out *Fallen Angels, Hoops, Motown and Didi*, and *Scorpions*.
1998 He travels with family to Holland and Germany.
1999 Myers begins writing for My Name Is America series.
2004 *Here in Harlem: Poems in Many Voices* is published.
2006 *Street Love, Jazz,* and *The Harlem Hellfighters: When Pride Met Courage* are published.

NOTES

Chapter 1

1. Tom Reynolds, "A Place Within Myself: Walter Dean Myers and the Fiction of Harlem Youth." NoveList Bibliographic Article. NoveList/EBSCO, 2005.

Chapter 2

2. Walter Dean Myers, *Bad Boy*. New York: HarperCollins, 2001, pp. 15–16.
3. "Autobiographical Sketch: Walter Dean Myers." EPA Top 100 Authors. EPA. www.edupaperback.org/showauth.cfm?authid=63.
4. Myers, *Bad Boy*, p. 46.
5. "Author Profile: Walter Dean Myers. In His Own Words." Teenreads.com. www.teenreads.com/authors/au-myers-walterdean.asp.
6. Myers, *Bad Boy*, p. 52.
7. Ibid., p. 7.

Chapter 3

8. Ibid., p. 126.
9. Ibid., p. 93.
10. Ibid., p. 111.
11. Ibid., p. 100.
12. Ibid., p. 153.
13. Ibid., p. 196.
14. Ibid., p. 179.

Chapter 4

15. "Author Profile: Walter Dean Myers. In His Own Words." www.teenreads.com/authors/au-myers-walterdean.asp.
16. Robert Lipsyte, "Fast Sam, Cool Clyde, and Stuff," *New York Times* (May 4, 1975): p. 280.

Chapter 5

17. "The Young Landlords," *Kirkus Reviews* (October 1, 1980).
18. Lou Willett Stanek, *A Study Guide on the Novels of Walter Dean Myers*. New York: Avon, 1980, p. 3.
19. Walter Dean Myers, *Motown and Didi*. New York: Viking Kestrel, 1984, p. 161.

Chapter 6

20. Donna Carrillo. "Walter Dean Myers Talks to Scholastic News Online." Scholastic News Online. http://216.182.167.201/scholasticnews/indepth/bullying/bullying_news/index.asp?article=waterdeanmyers2&topic=0.
21. Ibid.
22. Mel Watkins, "Fallen Angels," *New York Times* (January 22, 1989): p. BR28.
23. Shirley Horner, "Author Seeks to Inspire Black Youth,"

105

NOTES

New York Times (August 21, 1988): p. NJ10.

24. "Walter Dean Myers Interview." Scholastic.com. http://books.scholastic.com/teachers/authorsandbooks/authorstudies/.
25. "Walter Dean Myers Interview." HarperChildrens. http://www.harperchildrens.com/hch/parents/teachingguides/myers.pdf.
26. "Scorpions," *Kirkus Reviews* (May 15, 1988).
27. "Walter Dean Myers Interview." ReadingRockets. http://www.readingrockets.org/books/interviews/myersw/transcript.
28. Horner, "Author Seeks to Inspire Black Youth," p. NJ10.

Chapter 7

29. Walter Dean Myers, "Prologue," *Handbook for Boys*. New York: HarperCollins, 2002.
30. Walter Dean Myers, "I Actually Thought We Would Revolutionize the Industry," *New York Times* (November 9, 1986): p. BR50.
31. Stanek, *A Study Guide on the Novels of Walter Dean Myers*, p. 3.
32. Rudine Sims Bishop, *Presenting Walter Dean Myers*. New York: Twayne, 1991, p. 95.
33. Ibid., p. 94.
34. Horner, "Author Seeks to Inspire Black Youth," p. NJ10.
35. Carrillo. "Walter Dean Myers Talks to Scholastic News Online."
36. "Walter Dean Myers Interview." ReadingRockets.

Chapter 8

37. Kenneth C. Davis, "Many Rivers to Cross," *New York Times* (November 13, 1994): p. BR42.
38. Myers, *Slam!* New York: Scholastic, 1996, p. 1.
39. Ibid., p. 5.
40. "Walter Dean Myers Interview." Teenreads.com. www.teenreads.com/authors/au-myers-walterdean.asp.

Chapter 9

41. Carrillo, "Walter Dean Myers Talks to Scholastic News Online."
42. Myers, "I Actually Thought We Would Revolutionize the Industry," p. BR50.
43. Carrillo, "Walter Dean Myers Talks to Scholastic News Online."
44. Myers, *The Beast*. New York: Scholastic, 2003, p. 136.
45. Myers, *Blues Journey*. New York: Holiday House, 2003.
46. Jerry Gray, "He Knows I Have Come to Kill Him," *New York Times Book Review* (May 19, 2002): p. 35.
47. Ibid.
48. Carrillo, "Walter Dean Myers Talks to Scholastic News Online."
49. Sandy MacDonald, "Shooter," *New York Times Book Review* (September 19, 2004): p. 17.
50. "Walter Dean Myers Interview." Teenreads.com.
51. Carrillo, "Walter Dean Myers Talks to Scholastic News Online."

NOTES

52 "Author Profile: Walter Dean Myers. In His Own Words." Teenreads.com.

53 Carrillo, "Walter Dean Myers Talks to Scholastic News Online."

54 Ibid.

55 "Walter Dean Myers Interview." HarperChildrens.

56 Carrillo, "Walter Dean Myers Talks to Scholastic News Online."

57 Ibid.

WORKS BY WALTER DEAN MYERS

1969 *Where Does the Day Go?* (illustrated by Leo Carty)

1972 *The Dragon Takes a Wife*; *The Dancers*

1974 *Fly, Jimmy, Fly!*

1975 *The World of Work: A Guide to Choosing a Career*; *Fast Sam, Cool Clyde, and Stuff*

1976 *Social Welfare*

1977 *Brainstorm* (photographs by Chuck Freedman); *Mojo and the Russians*; *Victory for Jamie*

1978 *It Ain't All for Nothin'*

1979 *The Young Landlords*

1980 *The Black Pearl and the Ghost; or, One Mystery after Another*; *The Golden Serpent*

1981 *Hoops*; *The Legend of Tarik*

1982 *Won't Know Till I Get There*

1983 *The Nicholas Factor*; *Tales of a Dead King*

1984 *Mr. Monkey and the Gotcha Bird*; *Motown and Didi: A Love Story*; *The Outside Shot*

1985 *Adventure in Granada* (Arrow series); *The Hidden Shrine* (Arrow series)

1986 *Duel in the Desert* (Arrow series); *Ambush in the Amazon* (Arrow series); *Sweet Illusions*

1987 *Crystal*; *Shadow of the Red Moon*

1988 *Scorpions*; *Me, Mop, and the Moondance Kid*; *Fallen Angels*

1990 *The Mouse Rap*

1991 *Now Is Your Time! The African-American Struggle for Freedom*

1992 *Somewhere in the Darkness*; *Mop, Moondance, and the Nagasaki Knights*; *The Righteous Revenge of Artemis Bonner*; *A Place Called Heartbreak: A Story of Vietnam*

1993 *Malcolm X: By Any Means Necessary*; *Young Martin's Promise*; *The Test* (18 Pine Street series); *Fashion by Tasha* (18 Pine Street

WORKS BY WALTER DEAN MYERS

series); *Intensive Care* (18 Pine Street series); *Dangerous Games* (18 Pine Street series); *Brown Angels: An Album of Pictures and Verse*

1994 *The Glory Field*; *Darnell Rock Reporting*

1995 *The Story of the Three Kingdoms*; *Glorious Angels: An Album of Pictures and Verse*; *One More River to Cross: An African American Photograph Album*

1996 *Slam!*; *Smiffy Blue: Ace Crime Detective: The Case of the Missing Ruby and Other Stories*; *How Mr. Monkey Saw the Whole World*; *Toussaint L'Ouverture: The Fight for Haiti's Freedom* (paintings by Jacob Lawrence)

1997 *Harlem: A Poem* (illustrated by Christopher Myers)

1998 *Angel to Angel: A Mother's Gift of Love*; *Amistad: A Long Road to Freedom*

1999 *The Journal of Scott Pendleton Collins: A World War II Soldier,* (My Name Is America series); *The Journal of Joshua Loper: A Black Cowboy.* (My Name Is America series); *Monster* (illustrated by Christopher Myers); *Malcolm X: A Fire Burning Brightly*; *At Her Majesty's Request: An African Princess in Victorian England*

2000 *145th Street: Short Stories*; *The Blues of Flats Brown*

2001 *Bad Boy: A Memoir*; *The Greatest: Muhammad Ali*; *The Journal of Biddy Owens* (My Name Is America series); *Patrol: An American Soldier in Vietnam*

2002 *Handbook for Boys*; *A Time to Love: Tales From the Old Testament* (illustrated by Christopher Myers); *Three Swords for Granada*

2003 *The Beast*; *The Dream Bearer*; *Blues Journey*

2004 *Antarctica: Journeys to the South Pole*; *Here in Harlem: Poems in Many Voices*; *I've Seen the Promised Land: The Life of Dr. Martin Luther King, Jr.*; *USS Constellation: Pride of the American Navy*; *Shooter*

2005 *Autobiography of My Dead Brother* (illustrated by Christopher Myers)

2006 *Jazz* (illustrated by Christopher Myers); *The Harlem Hellfighters: When Pride Met Courage* (with William Miles); *Street Love*

POPULAR BOOKS

AUTOBIOGRAPHY OF MY DEAD BROTHER
Living in a neighborhood with a presence of gangs, drive-bys, and drugs, 15-year-old Jesse turns to his friends in "The Counts" for support. He feels as if he no longer knows his best friend, Rise, who has started dealing drugs. His search for the "old" Rise leads him to art. Jesse's illustrations and comic strip are the work of illustrator Christopher Myers.

BAD BOY: A MEMOIR
This memoir is about Myers growing up in Harlem. His vivid details bring the 1940s Harlem neighborhood to life. As Myers grows older, he struggles with the pressures of school and adolescence. Reading and writing are what save him from trouble.

THE BEAST
Anthony "Spoon" Witherspoon experiences a new life at a prep school in Connecticut. He hopes to go to college after he graduates. When he goes back to Harlem for Christmas break, he discovers that his beautiful poet girlfriend Gabi has turned to drugs. Now Spoon must save her from giving up her life to addiction.

CRYSTAL
This is one of Myers's few books that features a female protagonist. The main character is on her way to becoming a top model, but she must decide if she is willing to compromises her values. Crystal experiences many of the perks of modeling—hanging out with famous people and wearing beautiful clothes. She also witnesses the darker side to the profession: Will she find the courage to give up modeling?

FALLEN ANGELS
Myers wrote this novel as a tribute to his younger brother, who was killed in the Vietnam War. The story follows a young man's tour of duty in Vietnam in 1968. This novel is both a coming-of-age story and a story about the devastation of war. It received much critical acclaim, including the Coretta Scott King Award for Fiction.

POPULAR BOOKS

FAST SAM, COOL CLYDE, AND STUFF

This is Myers's first published novel. Four Harlem teenagers start "The Good People," a support network to help them deal with the problems they face in the neighborhood, at school, and at home.

THE GLORY FIELD

This novel follows the Lewises, an African American family, and spans nearly 200 years. It begins with young Muhammad Bilal's journey from Africa in 1753 and ends with a 1990s family reunion set on the plantation on Curry Island, South Carolina, where Muhammad was a slave. The novel traces several generations of the family, through the Civil War, the Depression, and the civil rights movement to the present day. This rich, sweeping novel celebrates African American experience and history through five central characters.

HOOPS

Seventeen-year-old Lonnie Jackson thinks basketball is the only thing he has going for him. When he and his troubled coach are offered large sums of money to shave points off a citywide basketball tournament championship game, Lonnie must draw on his sense of right and wrong to make the best decision.

IT AIN'T ALL FOR NOTHIN'

Tippy lives with his grandmother, but when she gets sick, he goes to live with Lonnie, his father. Tippy must chose between the values of his father, who lives a life of petty crimes, or his God-fearing grandmother. This sad, poignant novel portrays the pressures of growing up.

JAZZ

Myers teams up with his son Christopher to create a vibrant picture book about jazz. Myers's rhythmic poems and Christopher's bold pictures capture the many moods and sounds of jazz. This book appeals to all ages, both children and adults.

MONSTER

In this critically acclaimed novel, 16-year-old Steve is on trial for murder and could face the death penalty. Did Steve serve as a lookout in a drugstore robbery in which the owner was killed? Or was he just in the wrong place at the wrong time? Will Steve be acquitted? Is he the cold-blooded "monster" the prosecutor has portrayed him as?

POPULAR BOOKS

MOTOWN AND DIDI: A LOVE STORY

This is the first book Meyers wrote that uses the third-person point of view. Motown, who grew up in foster homes, tries to stay strong in the street of Harlem, while Didi dreams of escaping. After a violent episode, Didi and Motown team up against Touchy, the drug dealer in the neighborhood. They must turn to each other in order to survive the violence on the streets.

SCORPIONS

Myers wrote *Scorpions* in response to the growing presence of violence, gangs, and guns in the streets of American cities. As a 12-year-old in Harlem, Jamal Hicks faces many of these problems. Jamal's brother, the leader of a gang called the Scorpions, is in jail for murder, and now Jamal feels pressured to take over. When his brother's friend gives him a gun for protection, he takes it. Myers received many letters from teenagers when this book was published.

SHOOTER

Myers went to Littleton, Colorado, the site of the Columbine massacre, to research this novel. It is told from multiple perspectives in the aftermath of a Columbine-style rampage. Through a series of interviews with the shooter Leonard's best friend Cameron and his ex-girlfriend Carla, as well as newspaper clippings and the diary of Leonard, the story of Leonard's troubled life unfolds.

SLAM!

Seventeen-year-old Greg "Slam" Harris has transferred to a magnet school for the arts, a mostly white school. After being the hot shot star of his Harlem high school basketball team, he has to learn to be a team player at his new school. He must learn how to apply the confidence and determination he has on the court to the other parts of his life. Winner of the Coretta Scott King Award for Fiction.

WON'T KNOW TILL I GET THERE

Stephen Perry, 14, and Earl Goins, a troubled streetwise kid that Stephen's parents are considering adopting, are ordered by a judge to work in an old-age home after they are caught spray-painting graffiti on a subway car. The comical novel focuses on Stephen and Earl's road to becoming brothers and how they learn from the senior citizens.

POPULAR CHARACTERS

ANTHONY "SPOON" WITHERSPOON

In *The Beast*, sensitive and smart 17-year-old Spoon leaves Harlem to attend Wallingford Academy in Connecticut. He struggles to adjust to life at prep school and to survive the tensions of race and class. Nervous about what the future will bring, he is devastated when he returns to Harlem for Christmas break and discovers his girlfriend Gabi is hooked on drugs—known as the Beast. Spoon is observant and poetic. He learns much about the world and, despite the grim outlook, feels somewhat hopeful about the future.

CAMERON PORTER

Seventeen-year-old Cameron Porter was the best friend of Leonard Gray, who kills another student and then himself in *Shooter*. Cameron comes from a wealthy African American family and, on the outside, seems well adjusted. He is, however, lonely and does not have any close friends. He connected to Leonard, who did not fit in at school. Cameron does not realize how desperate and disturbed Leonard is until it's too late.

CRYSTAL

In *Crystal*, the title character enters the world of modeling after she is discovered when a commercial is filmed at her church. Crystal is sensitive, active in her church, and conflicted about the way her modeling career is going. She must deal with her agent, who exploits her youth, race, and sexuality. She also feels pressured by her mother to be a successful model. The modeling career takes a dark turn when Crystal feels like she is being asked to compromise her values.

DIDI

Frustrated by life in Harlem, Didi's dream is to get away and go to college in *Motown and Didi*. She struggles to deal with her mother's nervous breakdown, her brother's drug addiction, and the fact that her father abandoned the family when she was a child. Didi feels trapped by family problems and immense responsibilities. She falls in love with Motown, her refuge.

POPULAR CHARACTERS

GREG "SLAM" HARRIS

Seventeen-year-old Greg "Slam" Harris attends Larrimer Arts Magnet School in the book *Slam!* He is struggling with his grades and believes he doesn't fit in with the other students. He is worried that his buddy Ice is dealing drugs, and he is also upset because his grandmother is sick. Greg has a quick temper and is aggressive. He excels at basketball. On the court, he is confident and driven.

JAMAL HICKS

As the main character of *Scorpions*, 12-year-old Jamal is street-smart and quickly losing his childhood innocence—he is faced with pressures to run drugs, own a gun, and lead a street gang. Jamal also likes to draw and possesses a sweet gentleness. His best friend, Tito, is a sensitive dreamer. Jamal feels caught between these two worlds. When he takes a gun that is offered to him, the weapon makes him feel strong and respected, but the gun also leads to tragedy.

JESSE

In *Autobiography of My Dead Brother*, Jesse's closest friend is Rise, who is like a brother to him. Now he feels like he's losing Rise to the tough ways of the Harlem streets. Jesse, observant, artistic, and vulnerable, watches what is going down in his neighborhood—one friend carrying a gun, another dealing drugs, and another doing time in jail. To try to make sense of it all, Jesse turns to his art. Jesse is devoted to drawing and to his friends. He carries his sketchbook around with him to draw what he sees.

JIMMY LITTLE

Jimmy, the protagonist of *Somewhere in the Darkness*, is a bright and honest 14-year-old. He is having trouble in school, and things unravel when his father, Crab, a convicted criminal, shows up. Crab convinces Jimmy to go with him on a trip. Jimmy says good-bye to Mama Jean, the loving woman who has raised him, and accompanies his father on a trip that changes his life.

LONNIE JACKSON

In *Hoops*, Lonnie is finishing up his senior year and playing in a citywide basketball tournament. He is trying to figure out what to do with life. He is adrift and uncertain about the future. He is not getting along with his mother and is unsure if he should trust his coach, Cal Jones. Eventually, Lonnie and Cal develop a friendship. Lonnie wants to make something out of himself, and he realizes that he is confident in his ability to play basketball. In *The Outside Shot*, the

POPULAR CHARACTERS

sequel to *Hoops*, Lonnie must adjust to freshman life at Montclare State College in Indiana.

MOTOWN

Motown of *Motown and Didi* is a loner who grew up in a string of foster homes. Now he lives on his own in a burned-out building in Harlem and believes he only needs himself to depend on. He trusts very few people and has few friends. At night he works out to stay strong, and during the days, he looks for work. His closest friend is the Professor, an older man who owns a bookstore and acts as a father figure to Motown. When Motown meets Didi, they become friends. This friendship then blossoms into love.

RICHARD PERRY

Richard, the protagonist of *Fallen Angels*, is a Harlem teenager who enlists in the army because he can't afford college and wants to get out of the crime-ridden neighborhood. He soon finds himself in battle in the Vietnam War. Richard is thoughtful, curious, and compassionate. As he witnesses the violence of war, he questions many of his beliefs and ideas about the world. Richard is heroic, but he is also sensitive. He gains wisdom in this coming-of-age novel about himself and the adult world.

RISE

In *Autobiography of My Dead Brother*, Rise turns to dealing drugs and pulls away from his best friend Jesse. He is street-smart and brazen. Fearless, he taunts rival neighborhood gangs. He also deals coke on the street, wears flashy jewelry, and drives fancy cars.

STEVE HARMON

Steve, the 16-year-old star of *Monster*, is on trial for murder and could face the death penalty. During the trial, Steve feels disconnected. He pictures all the events as if he were directing a movie and decides to make a screenplay out of the experience. This helps him to distance himself from the frightening events.

STUFF

Twelve-year-old Francis, nicknamed "Stuff" for his nonexistent dunk shot, is the narrator of *Fast Sam, Cool Clyde, and Stuff*. He quickly becomes friends with Sam, Clyde, and Gloria, who start a group called "The Good People." Stuff describes himself as "kind of scary." He is easily scared and moved to tears. He is also bright, easygoing, and a good friend, "about the best listener around."

MAJOR AWARDS

1968 *Where Does the Day Go?* awarded first prize in a writing contest sponsored by the Council on Interracial Books for Children.

1972 *The Dancers* selected for the Child Study Association of America's Children's Books of the Year.

1975 *Fast Sam, Cool Clyde, and Stuff* selected for an ALA Notable Book.

1976 *Fast Sam, Cool Clyde and Stuff* awarded the Woodward Park School Annual Book Award.

1978 *It Ain't All for Nothin'* selected as an ALA Best Book for Young Adults and an ALA Notable Book.

1979 *The Young Landlords* selected as an ALA Notable Book and ALA Best Book for Young Adults.

1980 *The Young Landlords* awarded the Coretta Scott King Award for Fiction.

1981 *The Legend of Tarik* selected as an ALA Best Book for Young Adults and an ALA Notable Book.

1982 *Hoops* selected for the ALA Best Book for Young Adults and ALA Notable Book; *The Legend of Tarik* selected for the Notable Children's Trade Book in the Social Studies and the ALA Best Book for Young Adults; and *Won't Know Till I Get There* selected for the Parents' Choice Award.

1982 Myers awarded a National Endowment of the Arts grant.

1983 *Tales of a Dead King* selected for the New Jersey Institute of Technology Authors Award.

1984 *The Outside Shot* awarded the Parents' Choice Award.

1985 *Motown and Didi: A Love Story* awarded the Coretta Scott King Award for Fiction.

1987 *Adventure in Granada* selected for the Child Study Association of America's Children's Books of the Year citation.

1988 *Fallen Angels* selected as an ALA Best Book for Young Adults, an ALA Booklist Young Adult Editors' Choice, a School Library

MAJOR AWARDS

Journal Best Book of the Year, a Parents' Choice Award, the Horn Book Fanfare Honor List, and a Notable Children's Trade Book in the Field of Social Studies.

1988 *Scorpions* selected for an ALA Best Book for Young Adults, an IRA Young Adult Choice, and an ALA Notable Children's Book; *Me, Mop, and the Moondance Kid* selected for an ALA Notable Children's Book.

1988 Myers awarded for a MacDowell Colony Fellowship.

1989 *Fallen Angels* awarded the Coretta Scott King Award for Fiction; *Scorpions* selected as a Newbery Honor Book.

1989 Myers awarded a National Endowment of the Arts Grant.

1991 *The Mouse Rap*, selected for the IRA Children's Choice and ALA Best Book for Young Adults.

1992 *Now Is Your Time! The African-American Struggle for Freedom* awarded the Coretta Scott King Award for Nonfiction and the NCTE Orbis Pictus Award for Outstanding Nonfiction and selected for an ALA Best Book for Young Adults and Jane Addams Book Award Honor Book.

1992 Myers awarded the ALAN Award.

1992 *Somewhere in the Darkness* named a Coretta Scott King Honor Book and Boston Globe-Horn Book Honor Book.

1992 *The Righteous Revenge of Artemis Bonner* selected as an ALA Best Book for Young Adults and ALA Popular Paperback for Young Adults.

1993 *Somewhere in the Darkness* named a Newbery Honor Book, an ALA Best Book for Young Adults, an ALA Notable Children's Book, a Coretta Scott King Award Honor Book, an NYPL Book for the Teen Age, a School Library Journal Best Book of the Year, and an ALA Booklist Young Adult Editors' Choice.

1993 *Brown Angels: An Album of Pictures and Verse* selected as a *Parenting Magazine* 10 Best Book, an ALA Notable Children's Book, a Notable Trade Book in the Language Arts, and an NYPL Book for the Teen Age.

1994 *Malcolm X: By Any Means Necessary* named a Coretta Scott King Award Honor Book, an ALA Best Book for Young Adults, an ALA Notable Children's Book, an NYPL Book for the Teen Age, a Notable Children's Trade Book in the Field of Social Studies, and the IRA Teachers' Choice.

1994 Myers awarded the Margaret A. Edwards Award.

MAJOR AWARDS

1995 *The Glory Field* selected for an ALA Best Book for Young Adults, a Notable Children's Trade Book in the Field of Social Studies, and an NYPL Book for the Teen Age.

1997 *Slam!* awarded the Coretta Scott King Award and selected for an ALA Best Book for Young Adults; *Harlem: A Poem* named a Boston Globe-Horn Book Honor Book.

1997 *One More River to Cross* selected for an ALA Best Book for Young Adults and ALA Top 10 Best Book for Young Adults; *Toussaint L'Ouverture: The Fight for Haiti's Freedom* named an ALA Notable Children's Book.

1997 *Harlem: A Poem* selected as a Caldecott Honor Book, a Coretta Scott King Illustrator Honor Book, an ALA Best Book for Young Adults, and a Notable Children's Trade Book in the Field of Social Studies.

1997 *Malcolm X: A Fire Burning Brightly* selected for a Notable Children's Trade Book in the Field of Social Studies, a School Library Journal Best Book, and an NYPL 1,000 Titles for Reading and Sharing; *Harlem: A Poem* selected for a Boston Globe-Horn Book Award.

1999 Myers awarded the Virginia Hamilton Literary Award.

2000 *Monster* awarded the Michael L. Printz Award and selected as a Coretta Scott King Author Honor Book, a National Book Award Finalist, a Los Angeles Times Book Prize Finalist, a Boston Globe-Horn Book Honor Book, an ALA Best Book for Young Adults, and an NYPL Book for the Teen Age.

2000 *At Her Majesty's Request: An African Princess in Victorian England* named an NCTE Orbis Pictus Honor Book, a Notable Children's Trade Book in the Language Arts, a Notable Social Studies Trade Book for Young People, a BCCB Blue Ribbon Book, an NYPL 1000 Titles for Reading and Sharing, and an IRA Notable Book for a Global Society.

2000 *145th Street: Short Stories* selected for an ALA Best Book for Young Adults and a Boston Globe-Horn Book Award for Excellence in Children's Literature Honor Book.

2003 *Patrol* awarded the Jane Addams Peace Award.

2006 Myers selected as a Lacey Loves to Read author, Lacey, Washington.

BIBLIOGRAPHY

"Author Profile: Walter Dean Myers. In His Own Words," Teenreads. com. Available online. URL: www.teenreads.com/authors/au-myers-walterdean.asp.

"Autobiographical Sketch: Walter Dean Myers," EPA Top 100 Authors. EPA. Available online. URL: www.edupaperback.org/showauth.cfm?authid=63.

Bishop, Rudine Sims. *Presenting Walter Dean Myers.* New York: Twayne, 1991.

Carrillo, Donna. "Walter Dean Myers Talks to Scholastic News Online," Scholastic News Online. Available online. URL: http://216.182.167.201/scholasticnews/indepth/bullying/bullying_news/index.asp?article=waterdeanmyers2&topic=0.

Davis, Kenneth C. "Many Rivers to Cross." *New York Times* (November 13, 1994): p. BR42.

Gray, Jerry. "He Knows I Have Come to Kill Him." *New York Times Book Review* (May 19, 2002): p. 35.

Horner, Shirley. "Author Seeks to Inspire Black Youth." *New York Times* (August 21, 1988): p. NJ10.

Lipsyte, Robert. "Fast Sam, Cool Clyde, and Stuff." *New York Times* (May 4, 1975): p. 280.

MacDonald, Sandy. "Shooter." *New York Times Book Review* (September 19, 2004): p. 17.

Myers, Walter Dean. *Bad Boy.* New York: HarperCollins, 2001.

———. *The Beast.* New York: Scholastic, 2003.

———. *Blues Journey.* New York: Holiday House, 2003.

———. *Handbook for Boys.* New York: HarperCollins, 2002.

———. "I Actually Thought We Would Revolutionize the Industry." *New York Times* (November 9, 1986), p. BR50.

———. *Motown and Didi.* New York: Viking Kestrel, 1984.

———. *Slam!* New York: Scholastic, 1996.

BIBLIOGRAPHY

Reynolds, Tom. "A Place Within Myself: Walter Dean Myers and the Fiction of Harlem Youth." NoveList Bibliographic Article. NoveList/EBSCO, 2005.

"Scorpions." *Kirkus Reviews* (May 15, 1988).

Stanek, Lou Willett. *A Study Guide on the Novels of Walter Dean Myers.* New York: Avon, 1980.

"Walter Dean Myers Interview," HarperChildrens. Available online. URL: http://www.harperchildrens.com/hch/parents/teachingguides/myers.pdf.

"Walter Dean Myers Interview," ReadingRockets. Available online. URL: http://www.readingrockets.org/books/interviews/myersw/transcript.

"Walter Dean Myers Interview, February 4, 2000," Teenreads.com. Available online. URL: www.teenreads.com/authors/au-myers-walterdean.asp.

Watkins, Mel. "Fallen Angels." *New York Times* (January 22, 1989): p. BR28.

"The Young Landlords." *Kirkus Reviews* (October 1, 1980).

FURTHER READING

Burshtein, Karen. *Walter Dean Myers*. New York: Rosen, 2004.

Erlich, Amy, ed. *When I Was Your Age: Original Stories About Growing Up*. Cambridge, Mass.: Candlewick Press, 1996.

Garrett, A., and Helga P. McCue, eds. *Authors and Artists for Young Adults*, vol. 4. Detroit, Mich.: Gale, 1990.

Hamanaka, Sheila, ed. *On the Wings of Peace: Writers and Illustrators Speak Out for Peace, in Memory of Hiroshima and Nagasaki*. New York: Clarion Books, 1995.

Jordan, Denise M. *Walter Dean Myers: Writer for Real Teens*. Berkeley Heights, N.J.: Enslow, 1999.

Naughton, Jim. "Walter Dean Myers, Writing about Reality for Black Children." *Washington Post* (December 9, 1989): p. C01.

Patrick-Wexler, Diane. *Walter Dean Myers*. Austin, Tex.: Raintree Steck-Vaughan, 1996.

Sanchez, Sonia, ed. *We Be Word Sorcerers: Twenty-five Stories by Black Americans*. New York: Bantam, 1973.

Snodgrass, Mary Ellen. *Walter Dean Myers: A Literary Companion*. Jefferson, N.C.: McFarland, 2006.

Yunghans, Penelope. *Prize Winners: Ten Writers for Young Readers*. Greensboro, N.C.: Morgan Reynolds, 1995.

Web Sites

Educational Paperback Association
http://www.edupaperback.org/showauth.cfm?authid=63

"Learning About Walter Dean Myers"
http://www.scils.rutgers.edu/~kvander/myers.html

Web site of Teenreads.com
http://www.teenreads.com/authors/au-myers-walterdean.asp

PICTURE CREDITS

page:

10: AP Images, Henny Ray Abrams
14: Used by permission of HarperCollins. Photo by SMPhotography
18: AP Images
26: Sarah A. Bonner
29: Sarah A. Bonner
31: Sarah A. Bonner
34: © Bettmann/Corbis
41: AP Images
46: Sarah A. Bonner
56: Photo by Sandra Payne, courtesy Constance Myers
60: Used by permission of HarperCollins. Photo by SMPhotography
64: AP Images, David Handschu
68: Used by permission of HarperCollins. Photo by SMPhotography
74: Used by permission of HarperCollins. Photo by SMPhotography
80: AP Images, Peter Arnett
84: Constance Myers
92: Constance Myers

cover: Constance Myers

INDEX

African-American characters in fiction, 76, 89–90
    father-son relationship, 12, 51, 89
    importance of, 16, 76, 101
    Myers as pioneer of, 78
    realism of portrayals, 75–76
    scarcity of, 13, 36–37, 76–77
    as stereotypes, 54, 77
African Americans
    culture of, 21, 24, 37, 51, 52
    history of, in fiction, 89–90
    importance of role models for, 16, 76, 101
    magazines for, 51, 69
    Myers on being, 44
    photographs of, used as basis for text, 87–88
    writers, 13, 36, 44, 51, 52, 78
    See also Harlem, New York; racism
agents, 54
American Library Association (ALA)
    "Banned Books Week: Celebrating the Freedom to Read," 82–83
    Best Books for Young Adults, 61, 69, 86
    Booklist, 91
    Notable Books, 55, 58, 86–87
Amistad: A Long Road to Freedom (Myers), 15, 87
Angel: A Mother's Gift of Love (Myers), 88
Antarctica: Journeys to the South Pole (Myers), 94–95
At Her Majesty's Request: An African Princess in Victorian England (Myers), 53, 70
audio books, 88
Autobiography of My Dead Brother (Myers), 96
awards
    American Library Association Best Books for Young Adults, 61, 69, 86
    American Library Association Notable Books, 55, 58, 86–87
    Caldecott Honor Award, 27, 88–89
    Child Study Association of America's Children's Books of the Year, 53
    Coretta Scott King Awards, 12, 58, 62, 69, 86–87
    Council on Interracial Books for Children, 51
    Jane Addams Award, 96
    Life magazine competition, 42
    Margaret A. Edwards Award, 86
    Michael L. Printz Award, 91
    New York Public Library Books for the Teen Age, 87
    Newbery Honor Book Award, 12, 86
    Notable Children's Trade Book in Social Studies citation, 61
    Orbis Pictus Award for Outstanding Nonfiction, 87
    Parents' Choice Award, 62, 69
    received by Christopher, 27, 88–89
    Woodward Park School Annual Book Award, 55

Baldwin, James, 49
ballet, 52–53
Balzac, Honoré de, 42
banning books, 54, 82–83, 98
Baraka, Amiri, 51
baseball, 31–32, 59, 67
basketball, 36, 47, 50, 90
The Beast (Myers), 77–78, 94
Bishop, Rudine Sims, 78
Black Arts Movement, 51
blacks. *See* African-American characters in fiction; African Americans
Blues Journey (Myers), 27, 95
Bobbs-Merrill Publishing Company, 52, 55
Booklist (magazine), 91

INDEX

Brendel, Constance. *See* Myers, Connie (wife)
Brooke, Rupert, 44
Brown, John, 18–19
Brown Angels: An Album of Pictures and Verse (Myers), 87

Caldecott Honor Award, 27, 88–89
career as writer
    desire to have, 40, 43–44
    early, 11, 49, 54
    foster parents' influence on, 22–23
    full-time, 55, 57
    genres, 16, 51, 59, 63, 69, 85, 94, 101
    influential authors, 49
    lack of role models, 13, 36
    at MacDowell Colony, 89
    number of books published, 12, 65
    praise for, 80–82
    requirements for, 102
    work habits, 97–100, 99
    See also awards; inspiration sources
censorship, 54, 82–83, 98
Cherry, Fred V., 95
Child Study Association of America, 53
childhood
    appendicitis, 27
    education, 12, 24–25, 27–28, 30, 32–33
    in Harlem, 21–24
    in Martinsburg, 19–21
    reading as escape during, 12–13, 28, 30
    sports, 31–32
    stories written during, 30
    temper, 25
Children's Books of the Year award, 53
children's fiction, 59, 79
    See also picture books
Church of the Master, 32
City College of New York, 50
Columbia University, 51–52
Columbine High School massacre, 96–97
contests. *See* awards
Conway, Mrs., 27–28, 30
Coretta Scott King Awards, 12, 27, 58, 62, 69, 86–87, 88–89
Council on Interracial Books for Children, 51
Crystal (Myers), 76

The Dancers (Myers), 52–53
Davis, Kenneth C., 89–90
Dean, Florence Brown (foster mother)
    background of, 20–21
    death of, 53
    enlistment in Army and, 44
    name change and, 53
    in New Jersey, 48
    reading and, 22–23
    writing as career and, 40
Dean, Herbert (foster father)
    background of, 21–22
    death of, 63
    enlistment in Army and, 44–45
    name change and, 53
    in New Jersey, 48
    stories told by, 23
    writing as career and, 40
dialogue, 54, 72, 81–82, 94, 98
The Dragon Takes a Wife (Myers), 53–54

East Village, New York, 50
education
    college, 50, 59
    elementary school, 12, 24–25, 27–28, 30, 32–33
    high school, 38–39, 40, 42, 43
    writing courses/workshops, 49, 51–52
Empire State College, 59
employment. *See* career as writer; jobs
essays, 69, 101
Essence (magazine), 69

fables/fairy tales, 59
Fallen Angels (Myers), 67, 69, 82, 83, 98
Fast Sam, Cool Clyde, and Stuff (Myers), 13, 15, 54, 55, 82
fictional characters
    basis for and development of, 58–59, 81
    female main, 76
    language used by, 72, 74, 81
    white main, 38, 61
Finley, Mrs., 36
friendships
    interracial in books, 52–53, 77–78
    as teenager, 37–38, 42–43
    as theme, 76

INDEX

gangs, 43, 71
Giovanni, Nikki, 52
Glorious Angels: An Album of Pictures and Verse (Myers), 87
The Glory Field (Myers), 89–90
The Golden Serpent (Myers), 59
Great Depression, 20
The Greatest: Muhammad Ali (Myers), 94
gun proliferation, 71, 96–97

Hall, Frank, 42–43
Harlem: A Poem (Myers), 88–89
Harlem, New York
    African-American culture in, 21, 24, 32, 37, 51, 52
    as inspiration for fiction, 13, 16, 43, 71, 88–89
    move of biological father to, 35
    Myers on, 24–25, 27–28, 30, 32–33
    on own in, 48
    as setting for fiction, 32, 57–58, 61–63, 70, 94, 95, 97
The Harlem Hellfighters: When Pride Met Courage (Myers and Miles), 95
Harlem (Myers), 27
Harlem Renaissance, 37
Harlem Writers Guild, 52
Here in Harlem: Poems in Many Voices (Myers), 95
hobbies, 102
    See also reading; sports
honors. *See* awards
Hoops (Myers), 32, 61, 82
Hughes, Langston, 30–31

"I Actually Thought We Would Revolutionize the Industry" (Myers), 101
inspiration sources
    for characters, 58–59, 81
    life in Harlem, 13, 16, 43, 71, 88–89
    personal experiences, 63, 65–67, 69–70
interactive books, 63
It Ain't All for Nothin' (Myers), 57, 58
I've Seen the Promised Land: The Life of Dr. Martin Luther King, Jr. (Myers), 95

Jane Addams Award, 96
Jazz (Myers), 27
Jersey City, New Jersey, 66
jobs
    during Great Depression, 20
    held by foster father, 22
    held by Myers, 13, 40, 48, 49, 50, 52, 55
    See also career as writer
Jolly Brown Giants, 50

Killens, John O., 52
Kirkus Reviews, 58, 72

Lasher, Mr., 32–33
The Legend of Tarik (Myers), 59, 61, 67
Leonhardt, Eric, 37–38
Liebow, Mrs., 42, 43
Life (magazine), 42
Lipsyte, Robert, 55

MacDowell Colony, 89
Malcolm X: By Any Means Necessary (Myers), 87
Margaret A. Edwards Award, 86
marriages, 49, 50, 52
Martinsburg, West Virginia, 19–21
Me, Mop, and the Moondance Kid (Myers), 67, 77
Michael L. Printz Award, 91
Miles, Bill, 95
Mojo and the Russians (Myers), 57, 58
Monster (Myers), 79, 90–91
Morristown, New Jersey, 48
Motown and Didi: A Love Story (Myers), 43, 61, 62–63
movies from books, 53
Mr. Monkey and the Gotcha Bird (Myers), 63
Mushmouth, 25
music, 23–24, 50, 95
Myers, Christopher (son)
    as basis for fictional characters, 58–59
    birth of, 54
    as illustrator, 27, 79, 88–89, 95
    relationship with father, 66, 67, 100
Myers, Connie (wife), 16, 54, 55, 81, 100
Myers, Ethel (sister), 20

INDEX

Myers, George Ambrose (father), 20, 21, 35
Myers, George (brother), 20, 35
Myers, Geraldine (sister), 20, 21
Myers, Gertrude (sister), 20
Myers, Imogene (sister), 20
Myers, Joyce (wife), 49
Myers, Karen (daughter), 49, 59
Myers, Mary Dolly Green (mother), 20, 21
Myers, Michael Dean (son), 49, 55, 59, 66, 96
Myers, Sonny (brother), 67, 69
Myers, Viola (sister), 20, 21

name change, 53
National Council of Teachers of English, 87
National Enquirer (magazine), 51
New York State Department of Labor, 50
New York Times (newspaper), 69, 76–77, 89–90, 96, 97
Newbery Honor Book Award, 12, 86
The Nicholas Factor (Myers), 61, 66
nickname, 25
Notable Books (ALA), 55, 58, 86–87
Notable Children's Trade Book in Social Studies citation, 61

145th Street: Short Stories (Myers), 94
One More River to Cross: An African American Photograph Album (Myers), 88
Orbis Pictus Award for Outstanding Nonfiction, 87
The Outside Shot (Myers), 61

Parents' Choice Award, 62, 69
Parents' Magazine, 12, 51
Patrol (Myers), 95–96
photographs, books with, 87–88
picture books
  about Vietnam War, 95–96
  banned, 54
  early, 12, 13, 51
  illustrated by son Christopher, 27, 79, 95
  inspiration for, 63
  interracial friendships in, 52–53

modern fairy tale, 53–54
nonfiction, 87–88
praise for, 51, 53
A Place Called Heartbreak: A Story of Vietnam (Myers), 95
poetry, 30, 36, 87–88, 95
public library, 28, 87

Queens, New York, 50

racism
  awareness of, 37–38
  banned books and, 83, 98
  college and, 39
  in fiction, 15
  during Great Depression, 20
  Myers on friendship and, 38
reading
  efforts to encourage children, 101
  as escape, 12–13, 28, 30
  favorite childhood books, 30
  first books given to Myers, 28
  Myers on importance of, 102
  Myers on learning, 22–23
  Myers on love of, 28, 36
  speech impediment and, 25
  stigma of, 36
religion, 24, 32, 36
research projects, 66–67, 69, 87
Reynolds, Tom, 16

Scorpions (Myers), 69–73
segregation, 20, 39, 44
Shooter (Myers), 96–97
short stories, 94
Slam! (Myers), 77, 90
slavery, 15, 18–19
Smith, Joyce, 49
Somewhere in the Darkness (Myers), 89
speaking skills
  public speaking engagements, 100–101
  reading aloud own writing and, 30
  speech impediment, 12, 24–25, 33, 50
  speech therapy, 33, 50
  teaching and, 59
sports
  baseball, 31–32, 59, 67
  basketball, 36, 47, 50, 90

INDEX

boxers in Harlem, 30
writing about, 51, 90
"starving artist" period, 48–49
storytelling, 23
Stuyvesant High School, 38–39, 40, 42, 43
Sweet Illusions (Myers), 63

Tales of a Dead King (Myers), 53, 61, 66–67
Teachers & Writers Collaborative, 63
teenage years, 36, 38–39, 40, 42, 43, 44
"Telling Our Children the Stories of Their Lives" (Myers), 101
themes, 75–77, 90–91
Thomas, Dylan, 42
Toussaint L'Ouverture: The Fight for Haiti's Freedom (Myers), 87
travel, 66–67
True Romance (magazine), 22

U.S. Army, 44–48
U.S. Postal Service, 49, 50
USS Constellation (Myers), 94

Vietnam War, 67, 69, 95–96
violence
books about effects of, 69–73, 96–97
books about war, 67, 69, 96–97
books banned because of, 83, 98
by teenagers, 43, 70, 91

Watkins, Mel, 69
Where Does the Day Go? (Myers), 12, 51
Won't Know Til I Get There (Myers), 61–62
Woodward Park School Annual Book Award, 55

Yeh, Phoebe, 79
young adult fiction
about sports, 90
adventure, 59, 61
African-American family relations, 89
African-American writers of, 78
Arrow series, 38, 53, 61, 66–67
banned, 82, 83, 98
female main characters in, 76
first novel published, 13, 15, 54–55
Harlem as setting for, 32, 57–58, 61–63, 70, 94, 97
humor in, 53, 61–62, 78
language used, 54, 72, 81
movies from, 53
My Name is America series, 62
Myers' impact on teenagers, 72–73, 78–79
Myers on writing, 93–94
praise for, 58–59, 90–91
racial tensions in, 77–78, 94
realism of, 75–76
research for, 66–67
sequels, 61
use of third-person point of view, 62–63
violence in, 43, 67, 69–73, 96–97
white main characters, 38, 61
Young Adult Library Services Association, 86
young adult nonfiction, 15, 82, 87, 94–95
The Young Landlords (Myers), 53, 58, 66
Young Martin's Promise (Myers), 82, 87

ABOUT THE CONTRIBUTOR

AMY SICKELS lives in New York City. She received her MFA from Penn State University and has published stories and essays in literary journals, including *DoubleTake*, the *Greensboro Review* and the *Madison Review*.

B M996S
Sickels, Amy.
Walter Dean Myers /
CENTRAL LIBRARY
05/13

ICCRX

Friends of the
Houston Public Library